And the disciples came, and said unto him,
Why speakest thou unto them in parables?

He answered and said unto them,
Because it is given unto you to know
the mysteries of the kingdom of heaven,
but to them it is not given.

For whosoever hath, to him shall be given,
and he shall have more abundance:
but whosoever hath not,
from him shall be taken away
even that he hath.

Matthew 13:10-12

KEYS

— FOR —

INHERITING

— THE —

KINGDOM

UNLOCKING THE PARABLES OF JESUS

JAMES S. HOLLANDSWORTH

HOLLYPUBLISHING

The Bible version used in this publication
is the King James Version.

ISBN-10: 0-9963596-4-8
ISBN-13: 978-0-9963596-4-1

Printed in the United States of America.

Cover graphic design by Mark Oberkrom Design
Cover design idea by Anna Whiting (author's daughter) –
"The Pearl of Great Price," Matt. 13:45-46

Dedication

To my parents,
Jim and Marge Hollandsworth,
who have supported and encouraged me
in my pursuit of the kingdom.
I love you, Dad and Mom.
You contributed immensely
to the person I am today, by the grace of God.
I am so thankful for your example.

and …

To my parents in-law,
the late John Van Riper, Jr.
and his widow, Betty Ann Van Riper,
who adopted and raised Leslie,
the woman who became my lovely wife.
I am eternally grateful,
for I would be lost without Leslie.

Acknowledgements

Thank you, dear friends,
for willingly reviewing this book before publication,
and giving valuable input,
both theological and grammatical.
I greatly appreciate your wisdom and insight,
and I am honored by your friendship.

Keith Call
Marty Cauley
Tracy Daniels
John Sweigart
Todd Tjepkema

Contents

Chapter 1

Responding to
the Word of the Kingdom

Parable of the Four Soils
Matthew 13:1-23

Jesus was a master storyteller, frequently employing parables as a didactic tool when instructing His disciples. In fact, about one-third of His overall teaching was parabolic, drawing illustrations from everyday life for the purpose of driving home spiritual truths. Why did He use these clever little stories so often? As we shall see as we go along, He had an ulterior motive in addition to the more obvious one.

Bible scholars differ as to how many parables are recorded in the Scriptures. Depending on how one categorizes, the number ranges anywhere from two to three dozen. Still others count virtually every allegory used by Christ as a parable and therefore come up with a very long list of sixty-plus. My list is at the conservative end of the spectrum because: first, I do not view mere allegories as parables, and second, I believe Jesus began to speak deliberately in parables only at a certain point in His ministry, and He tells us so. That point is in Matt. 13. Thus, anything said before Matt. 13 — for example, the Sermon on the Mount, though it includes many allegories and metaphors — does not actually employ the use of parables. Christ's use of parables as a method of instruction starts in Matt. 13, and there is a reason for that, as we shall discover later in the chapter.

Rightly understanding the parables of our Lord is critical to understanding the deeper teaching of Jesus. But we have a bit of a hurdle. We live in the western world, where our natural tendency is to think more deductively and analytically. Whereas in the eastern world, the oriental mind is more given to thinking inductively, in figurative language, using metaphors and similes, allegories and word pictures, and even parables. We must remember that the Bible was not written by westerners; it was penned in the oriental world. The Middle East, as we refer to it, is oriental, not occidental. And so if we would understand the deeper truths of Scripture, which is oriental in style, we must reorient our minds (pun intended) to think in terms of the parabolic language frequently employed by Jesus. Most importantly, we must remember the audience to whom Jesus was speaking — first century Jews with an Old Testament psyche, not twenty-first century Gentiles with a New Testament grid. Otherwise, we will miss out on the depths of Christ's teaching, missing His point. It is, therefore, very important for students of the Word to seek the help of the indwelling Holy Spirit to illumine our understanding of the parables.

The Parables Are Non-Evangelistic

Parables are recorded only in the Synoptic Gospels — Matthew, Mark, and Luke. They are *not* included in John's Gospel. The word *parable* — Greek, *paroimia* — is used in John 10:6 in the King James Version. However, it is not the same Greek word used in the Synoptics, *parabole*. In John's Gospel the word means "adage" or "figure of speech," not *parable*. That is because John's Gospel is evangelistic. Its stated purpose is to convince the unsaved to believe that Jesus is the Christ the Son of God so that in believing they might have eternal life (see John 20:31).

I am writing on the presupposition that although John's Gospel is avowedly evangelistic, the focus of the Synoptics is *not* evangelistic. Their primary purpose is to point national Israel to repentance — turning from sin back to Jehovah — not to deal with matters of salvation from eternal condemnation. Thus, the Synoptics are directed at those who are already saved, focused on teaching the gospel of the kingdom, which is good news about the millennial kingdom for those who are saints. Understanding this hermeneutic (system of interpretation) is absolutely critical if one would unlock the parables. Once unlocked, the parables provide essential teaching for children of God as to how to inherit the kingdom.

So often the parables are "gospelized," which is the error of interpreting non-evangelistic passages as evangelistic (soteriological) passages, dealing with matters of salvation from eternal condemnation. Preachers and Bible teachers who make this grave mistake end up stealing from the saints passages that are intended to help prepare us to inherit the coming kingdom. When the parables are made out to be evangelistic texts, the correct interpretation is lost and saints remain unprepared to inherit the kingdom. In fact, those who hold to this erroneous hermeneutic typically assume all saints are automatic inheritors of the kingdom of heaven, which is also a grave mistake. More will be said about this later in the chapter. May we be careful to rightly divide the parables!

Parable #1: The Four Soils

1 The same day went Jesus out of the house, and sat by the sea side.

2 And great multitudes were gathered together unto him, so that he went into a ship, and sat; and the whole multitude stood on the shore.

3 And he spake many things unto them in parables, saying, Behold, a sower went forth to sow;

4 And when he sowed, some seeds fell by the way side, and the fowls came and devoured them up:

5 Some fell upon stony places, where they had not much earth: and forthwith they sprung up, because they had no deepness of earth:

6 And when the sun was up, they were scorched; and because they had no root, they withered away.

7 And some fell among thorns; and the thorns sprung up, and choked them:

8 But other fell into good ground, and brought forth fruit, some an hundredfold, some sixtyfold, some thirtyfold.

9 Who hath ears to hear, let him hear. Matt. 13:1-9

Notice that a man is planting seeds. As he throws them here and there and everywhere, they fall on four different types of ground:

1. **Wayside (v. 4)** — the footpath, which is so trampled down and hard there is no way the seed can take root. So the birds come and eat the seeds.

2. **Stony places (v. 5)** – rocky ground, where there is not much soil. The seed sprouts and grows a bit, but because of such little depth of soil, the plants cannot take root and they eventually wither and die in the heat of the sun.

3. **Thorny ground (v. 7)** – full of brambles. But because brambles are so invasive, they overpower the plants and choke them out.

4. **Good ground (v. 8)** – soil that is well-suited for growing things. There, the seed thrives and grows into healthy plants, producing fruit in varying quantities.

The parable of the four soils is frequently misinterpreted by many who say that one or more of these types of soils represent an unsaved, unregenerate person. As we've already indicated, the parables are not to be interpreted evangelistically. Jesus is not speaking about four types of responses to the gospel of salvation from Hell. We will demonstrate that fact very clearly in just a moment when we look at Christ's purpose for using parables.

Before Jesus gives the interpretation of the parable, His disciples ask an important question (v. 10): "Why do you speak in parables?"

Why Parables?

10 And the disciples came, and said unto him, Why speakest thou unto them in parables?

11 He answered and said unto them, Because it is given unto you to know the mysteries of the kingdom of heaven, but to them it is not given.

12 For whosoever hath, to him shall be given, and he shall have more abundance: but whosoever hath not, from him shall be taken away even that he hath.

13 Therefore speak I to them in parables: because they seeing see not; and hearing they hear not, neither do they understand.

14 And in them is fulfilled the prophecy of Esaias, which saith, By hearing ye shall hear, and shall not understand; and seeing ye shall see, and shall not perceive:

15 For this people's heart is waxed gross, and their ears are dull of hearing, and their eyes they have closed; lest at any time they should see with their eyes, and hear with their ears, and should understand with their heart, and should be converted, and I should heal them.
16 But blessed are your eyes, for they see: and your ears, for they hear.
17 For verily I say unto you, That many prophets and righteous men have desired to see those things which ye see, and have not seen them; and to hear those things which ye hear, and have not heard them. Matt. 13:10-17

We must remember that Jesus has been speaking to multitudes. From the context of Matt. 12, we know that some within the audience are scribes and Pharisees. All along they have been resistant to teaching about the kingdom of heaven, reaching back into the early chapters of Matthew's Gospel.

In those days came John the Baptist, preaching in the wilderness of Judaea, and saying, Repent ye: for the kingdom of heaven is at hand. Matt. 3:1-2

From that time Jesus began to preach, and to say, Repent: for the kingdom of heaven is at hand. Matt. 4:17

Both John the Baptist and Jesus had been preaching the message, *Repent ... for the kingdom of heaven is at hand.* Unfortunately, many preachers and Bible teachers have interpreted that statement to mean, "Get saved from eternal condemnation so you can go to Heaven when you die." But that is not what the message means. A first century Jew would have understood this message differently. The message actually means, "Turn from your sin so you can qualify to inherit the kingdom of the heavens."

Jehovah had promised Solomon that whenever sinning Israel would genuinely repent, God would forgive and restore the nation to fellowship, removing His hand of judgment.

If I shut up heaven that there be no rain, or if I command the locusts to devour the land, or if I send pestilence among my people; If my people, which are called by my name, shall humble themselves, and pray, and seek my face, and turn from their wicked ways; then will I hear from heaven, and will forgive their sin, and will heal their land. 2 Chron. 7:13-14

Hearing the call to repent by John and Jesus, Israelites of the first century would have been prompted to think of their sinfulness and God's divine judgment, already upon the nation in the form of Roman domination. Repentance in the spirit of 2 Chron. 7:14, would not only result in restoration but would qualify the nation to be included in the kingdom of the heavens, whatever that meant. That is how a first century Jew would have understood the message, in light of limited Old Testament revelation.

Convicted of their sin, multitudes responded favorably to the message and submitted to John's baptism of repentance. In fact, a revival of sorts broke out in Judea.

> And there went out unto him all the land of Judaea, and they of Jerusalem, and were all baptized of him in the river of Jordan, confessing their sins. Mark 1:5

Nevertheless, the arrogant religious leaders rejected John's message, assuming they were above it. They did not view themselves as sinful and worthy of divine judgment. Furthermore, they were skeptical of the concept of a *heavenly* kingdom. This was something new. From the Old Testament Scriptures they knew only of the *earthly* Messianic kingdom, and they knew, as Jews, they were guaranteed inclusion because of the promises of God. And so John the Baptist rebuked them.

> 7 But when he saw many of the Pharisees and Sadducees come to his baptism, he said unto them, O generation of vipers, who hath warned you to flee from the wrath to come?
> 8 Bring forth therefore fruits meet for repentance:
> 9 And think not to say within yourselves, We have Abraham to our father: for I say unto you, that God is able of these stones to raise up children unto Abraham.
> 10 And now also the axe is laid unto the root of the trees: therefore every tree which bringeth not forth good fruit is hewn down, and cast into the fire. Matt. 3:7-10

John essentially says, "You vipers, don't act as if you are repentant and right with God. Bring forth fruits that demonstrate you are truly right with God! And don't dare think that because you are of Jewish heritage that you will automatically inherit the heavenly realm of the kingdom. God is able of these stones to raise up children unto Abraham." The stones are likely a symbolic reference to the church of Jesus Christ. Then in v. 10 John warns of further temporal judgment that would come upon the nation for rejecting Christ's offer to co-rule in the heavenly realm of His kingdom. Indeed this prophecy was fulfilled in AD 70, when the Romans destroyed Jerusalem, including the temple.

Ironically, many twenty-first century Christian pastors and theologians are essentially proclaiming the same thing as the first century Jewish religious leaders: "We are guaranteed inclusion in the millennial kingdom on Earth." But John and Jesus aren't talking about the *earthly* kingdom of Messiah. They are preaching about how to qualify to be part of the *heavenly* kingdom, the ruling realm of the millennium, the heavenly Jerusalem. Inclusion in that realm is not automatic, based on Jewish heritage or salvation in Christ. Merely being saved doesn't guarantee that you are part of Christ's bride, His co-regent. Inclusion in the heavenly ruling realm is only for those saints who qualify through obedience and faithfulness, fulfilling the manner of living as mapped out by Jesus in the Sermon on the Mount, for example.

Many following Jesus have caught this truth, and they are continuing as disciples. By the way, disciples are not merely saved people. They are saved people who have chosen to follow Jesus in discipleship. They are paying the price to deny self and take up their cross and follow Him. There are many disciples in the multitude that are listening to Jesus in Matt. 13. But mixed into that crowd are also many who think they are guaranteed inheritors of the kingdom. They don't see a need to change, and assume they qualify automatically. The bottom line: They are not open to truth; they are unteachable; they are hard-hearted. This is what prompts Jesus to begin teaching using parables.

Revealing Truth While Concealing Truth

According to v. 11, Jesus wants those who are truly taking to heart what He has been saying to keep getting it, to grow deeper in their understanding of truth about how to prepare for the kingdom. On the other hand, He doesn't want those who are hard-hearted and resistant to His teaching to understand it. They have blocked Him out, so He will exclude them because of their unteachable spirit. In fact, according to v. 12, those who are grasping it because of their open heart and mind will be given truth more abundantly. Those who are resisting will have no desire to learn more; whatever truth they have heard will be taken from them. That is why Jesus is now resorting to speaking in parables (v. 13).

Parables are like coded language or keys of sorts. Only those who know the code or have the keys will be able to interpret the parables. Incidentally, the code is not reserved for some esoteric or elite group. It is available to any child of God who is genuinely seeking for truth, anyone with a teachable spirit. Parables, of themselves, are simple stories using everyday aspects of life to illustrate spiritual truth. But Jesus uses parables in a very specific manner to reveal truth to truth-seekers while concealing it from truth-rejecters, unteachable minds.

Isaiah predicted (Isa. 6:9-10) that some would be closed to truth. Jesus quotes the prophecy here in Matt. 13:14-15, applying it to first century Israel, and accusing the people of having fat hearts and heavy ears and closed eyes. They are deaf and blind and hard-hearted, not to mention hardheaded, and so the parables keep them from learning more. Ah, but the beauty of an open heart and mind (v. 16) is that it is "blessed."

Remarkably, we are told in v. 17 that the Old Testament prophets and patriarchs wanted to learn more about the kingdom of the heavens. Yet, God gave them only a tiny glimpse. For instance, Abraham *looked for a city which hath foundations, whose builder and maker is God*, Heb. 11:10. Moses *had respect unto the recompence of the reward*, Heb. 11:26. But God had not revealed to them the fullness of the heavenly New Jerusalem. Those truths remained hidden in the Old Testament era. Until the time of Christ's coming to Earth they were mysteries — the mysteries of the kingdom of heaven (v. 11). The mysteries have since been revealed by Christ through the medium of parables.

We are so blessed and privileged as New Testament era saints to have these truths revealed in our age. Think of it: The mysteries of the kingdom of heaven are now revealed for our understanding. Nevertheless, so many modern day Bible teachers have denied these truths are for saints, claiming, "We are children of God and therefore we expect to inherit all." It's essentially no different than the first century Jewish misunderstanding, "We have Abraham to our father." Twenty-first century teachers are stumbling over the parables just as first century leaders did. That's exactly what Jesus intended for those who resist truth. As we approach the parables of Christ, we must have open minds; we must be seekers of truth; and by all means, we must learn to interpret the parables correctly. To that end, Jesus gives the interpretation for the parable (Matt. 13:18-23).

The Interpretation

1. The Wayside Response

> Hear ye therefore the parable of the sower. When any one heareth **the word of the kingdom**, and understandeth it not, then cometh the wicked one, and catcheth away that which was sown in his heart. This is he which received seed by the way side. Matt. 13:18-19 (emphasis added)

The highlighted phrase in the above passage is key — *the word of the kingdom*. Notice it does not say *the gospel of salvation from eternal condemnation*. Again, the parables are not evangelistic. What is *the word of the kingdom*? The word *word* is *logos* in Greek. It is what is said about something. Specifically, in this case, it is what is said about the *kingdom*. What, in particular, had Jesus said about the kingdom? We already looked at that from Matt. 3. He said it was *at hand*, or we could say, "drawing near," in the sense that the kingdom of heavens was being offered. Jesus also spoke extensively of the qualifications for inheriting the kingdom in the Sermon on the Mount. *The word of the kingdom* is what Jesus said about qualifying to rule with Him in the heavenly ruling realm of the coming kingdom.

We must remember that inclusion in that realm is not automatic for Jews simply because of their heritage nor for Christians simply because they are children of God. One must qualify. When one hears this message, but does not under-stand it, then Satan snatches away the truth that was heard.

Why would someone not understand the message? More than likely, it is because they don't desire to understand it. The truth about the kingdom goes against everything they have been taught in their Bible college or church. They have always heard that *all* saints are automatically joint-heirs with Christ to co-rule with Him, guaranteed to inherit the king-dom. They have always assumed it to be one of the "blessings of salvation." But what they have never heard is that there are two realms of the kingdom: 1) *the earthly realm* that is guaranteed for all saints, and 2) *the heavenly realm* that is not guaranteed and for which one must qualify.

When they hear that truth, they short-circuit. They can't imagine it to be so, for they have never heard it. Perhaps they mock it or dismiss it. In that sense, they do not understand it. For whatever reason, their spiritual life is too shallow and immature to grasp the truth. And so Satan snatches away the truth and, very likely, because of their initial hardened reac-tion, they will never receive it. That is the response of the seed sowed on the wayside.

2. The Stony Ground Response

> But he that received the seed into stony places, the same is he that heareth the word, and anon with joy receiveth it; Yet hath he not root in himself, but dureth for a while: for when tribulation or persecution ariseth because of the word, by and by he is offended. Matt. 13:20-21

The seed sown on stony ground represents those who receive *the word of the kingdom* with joy and excitement. Their heart is open and teachable, they embrace it, taking off like a rocket, maybe even heralding the truth to others. However, in time, they are persecuted for believing *the word of the kingdom*, no doubt, by the wayside responders. Perhaps they are criticized for believing the parables are non-evangelistic. Maybe they are persecuted for taking the position that the parables are not merely for the Jews but for all believers desiring to understand the qualifications for inheriting the millennial kingdom. The pressure is too great, so they are offended. They stumble, capitulate, and leave off their embracing of kingdom truth. I would urge you, dear reader, not to respond in this way when folks ridicule you or ridicule your church for believing *the word of the kingdom*.

The typical form of ridicule is simply the allegation: "It's not biblical," or "This is heresy." Others might claim with great emotion: "I've never heard that in my entire Christian life, and I've been saved for forty years!" Though they might make these charges, they will typically not try to refute what you are saying with biblical arguments. They will simply use ad hominem arguments, emotional arguments, and blanket accusations. The bottom line is that they really don't know what they are talking about. Those who are ignorant often resort to blanket ridicule. The ridicule is too overwhelming for those who are not grounded well in *the word of the kingdom*, and so they wither and die with respect to this truth. That is the response of the seed sowed on stony ground.

3. The Thorny Ground Response

> He also that received seed among the thorns is he that heareth the word; and the care of this world, and the deceitfulness of riches, choke the word, and he becometh unfruitful. Matt. 13:22

Here we have another saint who is open-hearted and embraces *the word of the kingdom*. They understand the truth, and they grow in it. Thankfully, they are not thrown off track by those who love to persecute over this truth. However, something else causes them to stumble. Though they know the truth, *the care of this world and the deceitfulness of riches choke the word of the kingdom*, and they become unfruitful. Oh yes, they are saved, as are all the others, and they understand the truth about needing to qualify to inherit the kingdom. But they care more for the things of here and now than the things of eternity. They become worldly and unfruitful. They focus on the temporal and end up forfeiting their reward.

This is what John warned about when he said in 2 John 8, *Look to yourselves, that we lose not those things which we have wrought, but that we receive a full reward*. What a tragedy, for they know the truth, but they don't live the truth. That is the response of the seed sowed on thorny ground.

4. The Good Ground Response

> But he that received seed into the good ground is he that heareth the word, and understandeth it; which also beareth fruit, and bringeth forth, some an hundredfold, some sixty, some thirty. Matt. 13:23

There are some Christians who hear *the word of the kingdom*, receive it, embrace it, and get serious about living life for the glory of God and preparing for the kingdom. They become inheritors of the kingdom, for they are fruit-bearing saints, in varying amounts. They will enjoy the glories of the millennial kingdom and the eternal world to follow, for they will dwell with Christ in the heavenly Jerusalem and rule together with Him. Incidentally, that is the very purpose for which we were created. It is the ultimate way we glorify the Lord.

The Gospel of the Kingdom

The parable of the four soils reveals the common responses to Christ's teaching about the heavenly kingdom, referred to in Matt. 13:19 as *the word of the kingdom*. The four soils do not represent responses to the gospel of saving grace. Some disagree on the basis of the parallel passage in Luke 8, which gives another telling of the parable of the four soils. Luke, however, says it a bit differently.

> Those by the way side are they that hear; then cometh the devil, and taketh away the word out of their hearts, lest they should believe and be saved. Luke 8:12

Those who claim the parables are evangelistic point to this as one of their proof texts. But it is important not to haphazardly interpret this verse according to a particular theological system or tradition. We must also ask and answer the following questions: In the context, what is *the word*? What does it mean to *believe* this word? What does it mean to *be saved*?

In context, Jesus is preaching the *gospel of the kingdom* to national Israel, encouraging the nation to repent lest they face temporal judgment — which did, indeed, come upon Israel in AD 70 at the hand of the Romans. The message of the gospel of the kingdom is the good news that a new heavenly realm of the kingdom is now being announced, after remaining a mystery in the Old Testament. This new heavenly realm is referred to as *the kingdom of the heavens*, the ruling realm of the Messianic kingdom — the headquarters, if you will — from which Christ will rule over Heaven and Earth along with His co-regent, His bride.

In the Old Testament, national Israel had already been promised rule over the Gentile nations in the *earthly* Messianic kingdom, but this is a new offer of inclusion in the *heavenly* realm, the privilege of co-ruling with Christ. However, it is not automatic, for those who co-rule with Jesus must qualify to be His bride and co-regent. Those who live in the manner described in the Sermon on the Mount, for example, will inherit the kingdom of the heavens. That's the good news. All other saints will be relegated to the relative darkness outside, the *earthly* realm of the kingdom. That's the bad news.

This good news, with its corresponding bad news, comprises the *gospel of the kingdom*, otherwise known as *the word of the kingdom*. Again, this has nothing to do with salvation from eternal condemnation. Thus, in this context, the *word* (*logos* in the Gr.) is *the word of the kingdom*, Christ's teaching about the kingdom of the heavens. Those who *believe* the word of the kingdom are those who repent and bring forth the fruits of repentance. Incidentally, the word *believe* is a participle, and is correctly translated in Young's Literal Translation, *lest having believed, they may be saved*. The word *saved*, then, in this context is not about the salvation of one's spirit from eternal Hell. It is the salvation of the soul, resulting in reward at the Judgment Seat.

> Now after that John was put in prison, Jesus came into Galilee, preaching the gospel of the kingdom of God, and saying, The time is fulfilled, and the kingdom of God is at hand: repent ye, and believe the gospel. Mark 1:14-15

The mistake of many is to assume that believing the gospel in this passage, as in the Luke 8:12 passage, means believing the message of salvation by grace through faith alone. But that is not contextual. Again, the *gospel* in this context (referred to as *the word* in Luke 8:12) is *the gospel of the kingdom*, otherwise known as *the word of the kingdom*, not *the gospel of grace* (eternal salvation by faith alone). Believing the gospel of the kingdom is not the same as believing the gospel of grace. The gospel of the kingdom is for those already saved and pertains to sanctification and reward. The gospel of grace is for those who are lost and pertains to justification and eternal life. They are different messages, intended for different audiences.

In what sense, then, do those who believe the gospel of the kingdom become *saved* (Luke 8:12)? For the first century Jews, it means they will be delivered from impending destruction at the hand of the Romans. For Christians of the church age, it means they will be delivered from self-destruction now and from negative reward at the Judgment Seat.

What type of ground are you? Assuming you are a child of God, how are you presently responding to the gospel of the kingdom? Are you preparing to inherit the kingdom of the heavens?

Chapter 2

The Enemy Strikes Back

Parable of the Wheat & Tares
Matthew 13:24-30, 36-43

Satan's objective is to keep saints from understanding the word of the kingdom — truth about the need to qualify to inherit the heavenly ruling realm of the kingdom — lest they believe the message, repent of (i.e., turn from) their sins and start living a holy life unto the Lord. Satan does not want believers to be rewarded at the Judgment Seat as *sons unto glory* (Heb. 2:10). His primary mission is keeping saints from hearing and believing the word of the kingdom. But what happens when children of God believe and embrace the word of the kingdom? What is Satan's "Plan B," so to speak? That is what we will discover in the second parable.

Parable #2: The Wheat and Tares

24 Another parable put he forth unto them, saying, The kingdom of heaven is likened unto a man which sowed good seed in his field:
25 But while men slept, his enemy came and sowed tares among the wheat, and went his way.
26 But when the blade was sprung up, and brought forth fruit, then appeared the tares also.

27 So the servants of the householder came and said unto him, Sir, didst not thou sow good seed in thy field? from whence then hath it tares?
28 He said unto them, An enemy hath done this. The servants said unto him, Wilt thou then that we go and gather them up?
29 But he said, Nay; lest while ye gather up the tares, ye root up also the wheat with them.
30 Let both grow together until the harvest: and in the time of harvest I will say to the reapers, Gather ye together first the tares, and bind them in bundles to burn them: but gather the wheat into my barn. Matt. 13:24-30

Typically, commentators will make the claim that *the kingdom of heaven* is Heaven, the *good seed* is the gospel of salvation by grace through faith alone, the *wheat* are Christians, and the *tares* are the unsaved who profess to be Christians. Those who hold to this position often say this is a picture of the kingdom in mystery, that is, a picture of how the kingdom exists in the present age in spiritual form (as God sees it) while awaiting the coming literal kingdom. In other words, it shows how the visible church is comprised of true believers and nominal believers, mere professors of salvation who are not really saved. Though that is the common interpretation, I believe it is wrong and fraught with problems. To arrive at a correct understanding we must read Christ's interpretation in vs. 36-43:

36 Then Jesus sent the multitude away, and went into the house: and his disciples came unto him, saying, Declare unto us the parable of the tares of the field.
37 He answered and said unto them, He that soweth the good seed is the Son of man;
38 The field is the world; the good seed are the children of the kingdom; but the tares are the children of the wicked one;
39 The enemy that sowed them is the devil; the harvest is the end of the world; and the reapers are the angels.
40 As therefore the tares are gathered and burned in the fire; so shall it be in the end of this world.
41 The Son of man shall send forth his angels, and they shall gather out of his kingdom all things that offend, and them which do iniquity;
42 And shall cast them into a furnace of fire: there shall be wailing and gnashing of teeth.
43 Then shall the righteous shine forth as the sun in the kingdom of their Father. Who hath ears to hear, let him hear. Matt. 13:36-43

Both wheat and tares are saved people. There are no unbelievers here. How do we know this? First, consider that in vs. 28-29, the servants are told not to gather up the tares before the harvest, lest they uproot the wheat also. If the wheat are saved folks, and the tares are unsaved, then how would removing the unsaved imposters prematurely uproot the saved? The saved are eternally secure; nothing can uproot them. So the imagery of uprooting makes no sense if the wheat are saved and the tares are unsaved.

Second, notice the purpose of the parable in v. 24, "The *kingdom of heaven* is like ..." Once again, Jesus is describing some aspect of the kingdom of the heavens. As in the previous parable, He doesn't describe the kingdom proper, in the sense of the place or the realm. Rather, He describes how people will respond to the *word* of the kingdom — the proffered message of the kingdom — including Satan's opposition to it. That is the context of all the parables in Matt. 13. In fact, v. 19 is the hinge of sorts on which all the parables in this chapter swing open.

> When any one heareth **the word of the kingdom**, and understandeth it not, then cometh the wicked one, and catcheth away that which was sown in his heart. This is he which received seed by the way side. Matt. 13:19 (emphasis added)

How will hearers respond to the word of the kingdom, also known as the gospel of the kingdom? Furthermore, how will the word of the kingdom fare in the present age? What will Satan do to keep the message from spreading? These questions sum up the focus of the seven parables in Matt. 13.

Satan's Counterfeits

In this second parable, the wheat and tares, Jesus is teaching that the word of the kingdom message will be counterfeited by Satan. How will this happen? According to vs. 37-38, Jesus goes throughout the world sowing good seed. The good seed are children of the kingdom. Interestingly, the Greek word Jesus chooses for *children* is not *teknon*, the Greek word used to describe sons in general, but rather it is *huios*, the Greek word used to describe mature sons, those who are qualifying to become adopted as firstborn heirs to rule with Christ. These are not merely saved people, but those saints who have embraced the word of the kingdom message in the parable of the four soils. They are the "good-ground responders," those who are bearing fruit.

As Jesus plants sons unto glory throughout the world — those who believe the gospel of the kingdom message and are actively preparing for the kingdom — Satan comes along covertly and sows tares. The tares, a type of weed known in the Middle East as darnel, look nearly identical to the wheat. Nevertheless, there is a big difference. The wheat is fruit-bearing and profitable; the tares are non-productive, invasive, and even toxic if consumed. These tares may be kingdom of heaven look-alikes, but they are actually counterfeits who oppose the children of the kingdom. This does not mean they are unbelievers trying to infiltrate the church. Quite the contrary, they are believers whom Satan uses in an attempt to stop the fruitfulness of the children of the kingdom, the sons unto glory. We must keep in mind: These parables are not about how the gospel of grace fares in the present age, but how the word of the kingdom fares.

Yes, the tares are referred to as *the children of the wicked one* in v. 38, but this does not mean they are unsaved. Rather, they are saints — in fact, Christian leaders, pastors and teachers — who have been deceived by Satan to preach a message that is strikingly similar to the word of the kingdom, but not quite accurate. It is a counterfeit. Just as the Jewish leadership at the time of Christ misunderstood and refused His offer of the kingdom, so these Christian leaders in our day are primarily the ones misunderstanding and refusing Christ's offer to rule with Him in the kingdom of the heavens.

Some may be troubled to think that the term, *children of the wicked one,* could be referring to saints, but did not Jesus say to Peter, *Get thee behind me, Satan*, Matt. 16:23? The point is that whenever a child of God is deceived and being used as a tool of Satan to spread error, he or she is functioning as a child of the wicked one. Children of God can act like children of the devil, and when they do, they are *called* his children, in terms of their behavior, because of the way they are acting. On the flipside when positional children of God act as His children,

He *calls* them children in terms of their behavior. In fact, this is held up as a reward in Matt. 5:9, *Blessed are the peacemakers: for they shall be called the children of God*. It is quite possible for a positional child of God to behave like a child of the devil and thereby become identified with the wicked one in terms of their behavior.

When I was a child, I would sometimes play with a neighbor boy whose last name was Flanagan. We lived in an Irish neighborhood on the south side of Chicago. Whenever I played with the Flanagan boy, I would start acting like him, but he was not very well behaved. I remember my father saying, "You are a Hollandsworth. Make sure you act like a Hollandsworth, not like a Flanagan!" How many children of God are acting like children of the devil? They don't belong to Satan, but when they submit to his will, rather than God's will, they start acting like the devil's child. The tares in the second parable are called *children of the wicked one* because they believe and teach Satan's counterfeit message about the kingdom, rather than the message of truth as taught by Christ.

Satan is desperate to stop children of God from becoming children of the kingdom. His objective is to hinder saints from progressing all the way to maturity in discipleship. Thus, he starts by preventing them from understanding the gospel of the kingdom, as we saw in the parable of the four soils. But if that fails, he then goes to Plan B, seeking to stop those who believe the word of the kingdom from progressing in fruit-bearing. He does that by planting a counterforce who oppose the gospel of the kingdom message and thereby minimize the effectiveness of the children of the kingdom in this world.

The Methods of Counterfeiting

How do Christian leaders counterfeit the word of the kingdom? They do so, usually unwittingly, in at least four ways.

1. **Diluting the doctrine of eternal rewards.** Commonly taught by many Christian leaders is that saints have nothing of a negative nature to worry about at the Bema (Judgment Seat of Christ) because sin has all been forgiven at Calvary. The Bema is typically described as an awards ceremony, with

all saints being rewarded in some degree. They claim there is no prospect of judgment or punishment for unfaithful, carnal saints, even though the event is called the *Judgment* Seat. In fact, many who hold to this view turn to Greek cultural usage to define the word *Bema,* as the podium for dispensing rewards at the olympic games, despite the fact that the word is never used in that sense in the Bible. In the Scriptures, the Bema was the official judgment seat of magistrates, from which they would dispense both positive and negative verdicts. Jesus was condemned to death by Pilate on his Bema seat!

Those who dilute the biblical doctrine of eternal rewards implicitly condone licentious living. Think about it. If there is no possibility of negative consequence when we meet Jesus, then maybe it really doesn't matter how we live our lives now. Is that not the logical conclusion? A fundamentalist pastor told me that the prospect of negative reward at the Judgment Seat is "preposterous, for what motivates us is love for Christ, not fear!" I could not help thinking of my children's behavior when they were young. They didn't obey out of love; they obeyed out of fear of punishment! As they matured, however, they learned to obey out of love. The average Christian is not mature enough to obey the Lord out of love. Their obedience needs to be motivated by *the terror of the Lord*, 2 Cor. 5:11. Perhaps in time they will learn to obey Him because they love Him and desire to be rewarded by Him. But even in maturity, we sometimes get out of line and need to be reminded, *Our God is a consuming fire*, Heb. 12:29.

I wrote a previous book on the doctrine of eternal rewards, *The End of the Pilgrimage: Your Judgment Seat Verdict and How It Determines Your Place in His Kingdom*. I would encourage you to consult that book for further information on the subject. Nevertheless, diluting the doctrine of eternal rewards is one way Christian leaders counterfeit the word of the kingdom.

(2.) **Assuming all saints will rule and reign with Jesus.** Some like to refer to this as one of the "blessings of salvation," considering it automatic for all believers. Nothing could be further from the truth. Careful students of the Scripture will notice that God puts conditions on rulership. One must meet His conditions if they would rule.

3. **"Gospelizing" much of the New Testament.** This is the hermeneutical error of presuming the Synoptic Gospels and much of the rest of the New Testament are focused on the gospel of grace by which we are saved. Those who approach the Scriptures through this lens tend to preach gospel messages frequently in their churches, thereby keeping the saints in immaturity. The preponderance of Scripture, including the content of the Synoptic Gospels, is intended for the sanctification of saints, not the salvation of the lost.

4. **Focusing almost exclusively on "soulwinning" to the exclusion of discipleship and preparing sons unto glory.** I do not believe Satan is as intimidated by the salvation of lost people as he is the progression of saints in discipleship, those who are qualifying as firstborn sons to inherit the heavenly kingdom and rule with Jesus over the angelic realm and over mankind in the coming kingdom. Please don't misunderstand. Telling unbelievers the wonderful news of salvation from eternal condemnation through Jesus Christ is critically important. That is where life begins. But when that is the all-consuming goal of the church, to the extent that sanctification of believers becomes second fiddle, then something is dreadfully wrong. The church has wrong priorities. Ponder the magnificence of 1 Cor. 2:5-9.

> 5 That your faith should not stand in the wisdom of men, but in the power of God.
> 6 Howbeit we speak wisdom among them that are perfect: yet not the wisdom of this world, nor of the princes of this world, that come to nought:
> 7 But we speak the wisdom of God in a mystery, even the hidden wisdom, which God ordained before the world unto our glory:
> 8 Which none of the princes of this world knew: for had they known it, they would not have crucified the Lord of glory.
> 9 But as it is written, Eye hath not seen, nor ear heard, neither have entered into the heart of man, the things which God hath prepared for them that love him. 1 Cor. 2:5-9

What is the wisdom of God that was hidden in Old Testament times, but was later revealed and taught by Paul to those who are perfect (mature)? It is the wisdom that is *unto our glory* (v. 7). In other words, Paul was teaching the gospel of the kingdom, the word of the kingdom, the good news that those who prepare to be sons unto glory will have the privilege of reigning with Christ in His kingdom, wearing the crowns formerly held by Satan and his horde.

The princes of this world — that is, Satan and the fallen angels (John 12:31; 14:30; 16:11) — did not know of this glorious plan when driving Jesus to the cross. They did not know that God had a strategy to prepare certain chosen ones out of the redeemed to rule with the resurrected Jesus over Satan's kingdom. Had they known this, they would never have crucified Jesus, the Lord of glory! For those who love Jesus, on the other hand, they have in store something they cannot begin to imagine. The divine blueprint is truly brilliant!

What does this suggest about those church ministries that are so focused on reaching the unsaved that they have largely lost sight of reaching the saved? The word of the kingdom is a tremendous threat to Satan. It is no wonder he is diligently at work counterfeiting the message to stop Christians from bearing fruit.

By diluting the doctrine of eternal rewards, assuming that all saints will rule with Jesus, gospelizing the Synoptic Gospels, and focusing almost exclusively on "soulwinning," Christian leaders are functioning as tools of Satan, tares amongst the wheat. To the extent that is happening in the church of Jesus Christ, saints are not being prepared to rule with Jesus. They are missing the mark, ignoring the great purpose for which we were created. Inheritance is being forfeited with the end result that God is not glorified. What a tragedy!

Thus, the tares are Satan's tools within Christianity, his agents on the inside, Christian leaders who are unwittingly counterfeiting the word of the kingdom and thereby teaching error. The end result of their erroneous doctrine is that saints are held back from bearing fruit and qualifying to inherit the kingdom. This is how the enemy strikes back.

Judgment at the End of the Age

We come now to the final part of the parable, judgment at the end of the age.

> 39 The enemy that sowed them is the devil; the harvest is the end of the world; and the reapers are the angels.

40 As therefore the tares are gathered and burned in the fire; so shall it be in the end of this world.

41 The Son of man shall send forth his angels, and they shall gather out of his kingdom all things that offend, and them which do iniquity;

42 And shall cast them into a furnace of fire: there shall be wailing and gnashing of teeth.

43 Then shall the righteous shine forth as the sun in the kingdom of their Father. Who hath ears to hear, let him hear. Matt. 13:39-43

Typically, those who refuse to accept the word of the kingdom stumble over this point more than any other. They insist the fire is a picture of Hell for unbelievers. But notice that the judgment here for both wheat and tares occurs at the *same time*, at the end of *this* age: v. 39, *the harvest is the end of the world* (age); and v. 40, *so shall it be in the end of this world* (age). Therefore, the tares absolutely cannot refer to the unsaved, for the Scriptures are clear that judgment of unbelievers takes place *after* the millennium (Rev. 20:11-15), a thousand years after the end of this age. <u>The fact that wheat and tares are judged together in this parable is clear indication they are all believers. No unbelievers are being judged in this parable</u>.

A more suitable explanation for the fire in this text is that it refers to the Judgment Seat fire. Consider the following passages:

If a man abide not in me, he is cast forth as a branch, and is withered; and men gather them, and cast them into the fire, and they are burned. John 15:6

Every man's work shall be made manifest: for the day shall declare it, because it shall be revealed by fire; and the fire shall try every man's work of what sort it is … If any man's work shall be burned, he shall suffer loss: but he himself shall be saved; yet so as by fire. 1 Cor. 3:13, 15

But that which beareth thorns and briers is rejected, and is nigh unto cursing; whose end is to be burned. Heb. 6:8

All of these passages refer to the fire of the Judgment Seat that will test our works, not Hell or the lake of fire. The tares will be hurt by the Judgment Seat fire, that is, their works will be entirely consumed. In this context, the tares are Christian leaders unwittingly used by Satan to counterfeit the word of the kingdom. The terrible consequence of promulgating error will be *weeping and gnashing of teeth,* an oriental expression of sorrow and deep regret. More will be said about this term in Chapters 9, 10 and 12.

The *works* of these Christian leaders — including their *words,* their doctrine — will be put on trial and will come up short. They will burn up! Teaching Satan's counterfeit message, criticizing the word of the kingdom, and persecuting or separating from those who teach it are all serious, punishable offenses. One day they will regret having an unteachable spirit, despite being given many opportunities to consider the truth of the kingdom.

Perhaps the tares will be among those who cry out for God's mercy at the Judgment Seat:

> Many will say to me in that day, Lord, Lord, have we not prophesied in thy name? and in thy name have cast out devils? and in thy name done many wonderful works? Matt. 7:22

A modern version might be, "Lord, we held to the fundamentals of the faith. We preached the gospel and separated from worldliness and offered numerous ministries in our church. We had a Christian school and an awesome music program and an addictions recovery program, and we supported missions." How will our Lord respond to this passionate plea? He will declare to them, *I never knew you: depart from me, ye that work iniquity,* Matt. 7:23.

How could Jesus say, "I never *knew* you" to a child of God? The Greek verb translated *know* in the verse is *ginosko.* It means to have intimate, experiential fellowship with someone. Tragically, many believers are God's children but never experience closeness of fellowship with Him. Those who promulgate the counterfeit message of Satan, opposing the word of the kingdom as tares amongst the wheat, are not in closeness of fellowship with the Lord. How can they be, if they are teaching a message that is contrary to God's will? Indeed, Jesus says:

> Not every one that saith unto me, Lord, Lord, shall enter into the kingdom of heaven; but he that doeth the will of my Father which is in heaven. Matt. 7:21

The will of the Father is that we prepare for the kingdom personally while teaching the word of the kingdom to other saints as well. Those who are doing so will inherit the heavenly kingdom. Those who are not doing so, despite their cries for mercy, will not inherit the kingdom.

In Matt. 7 Jesus says, *Depart from me*. In Matt. 13 He says, *Cast them in a furnace of fire*. In Matt. 25 He says, *Cast the unprofitable servant into outer darkness*. These are synonymous terms, describing the same thing: removal from the ruling presence of Jesus, the heavenly New Jerusalem. Some might attempt to argue that believers cannot be *cast out* on the basis of John 6:37:

> All that the Father giveth me shall come to me; and him that cometh to me I will in no wise cast out. John 6:37

In the context of John 6 Jesus is referring to eternal security. His point is that believers cannot become unbelievers. That is, they cannot perish in Hell or be taken out of a saving relationship as children of the Father. However, in the context of our parable in Matt. 13, Jesus is referring, not to eternal salvation from Hell, but eternal *reward*. His point here is that believers can be disinherited from the heavenly ruling realm of the kingdom, while remaining in the kingdom.

In contrast, what happens to the wheat, the fruit-bearing children of the kingdom? They are abundantly rewarded!

> Then shall the righteous shine forth as the sun in the kingdom of their Father. Who hath ears to hear, let him hear. Matt. 13:43

A Right Response to Tares

What a wonderful promise! What, then, should be our response to this parable? First, with respect to ourselves, *take heed! Who hath ears to hear, let him hear*. Second, with respect to the tares amongst us, how should we respond?

> The servants said unto him, Wilt thou then that we go and gather them up? But he said, Nay; lest while ye gather up the tares, ye root up also the wheat with them. Let both grow together until the harvest: and in the time of harvest I will say to the reapers, Gather ye together first the tares, and bind them in bundles to burn them: but gather the wheat into my barn. Matt. 13:28b-30

We are to respond to the tares — those who refuse the word of the kingdom and perhaps criticize it or persecute those who hold to it — by leaving them alone. Ignore them. Let God sort them out in the harvest at the end of the age. It is not your duty to change them. You are called to be faithful in your lifestyle and to preach the truth. Beyond that, don't single out those who oppose. Don't criticize them, don't argue with them, don't write about them on your blog, don't pester them. Simply leave them in God's hands. He will deal with them at the Judgment Seat.

We are told why we should leave them alone: Lest we uproot some wheat when uprooting tares. As mentioned earlier, this cannot be referring to merely saved people, for saved people are eternally secure and cannot be uprooted. This must be referring to children (Gr. *huios*, mature sons) of the kingdom, for they can be uprooted so that they stop following the Lord. Perhaps one way they can become up-rooted is by our refusal to leave alone those who resist the word of the kingdom. If we get into ugly, back-and-forth argument with those who resist this truth, children of the kingdom may get caught in the crossfire and sickened by it and leave off their belief in this truth because of our ugliness. So leave them alone until the day of harvest when God will make all things right. He that hath ears to hear, let him hear.

Chapter 3

A Completely Leavened Church

Parables of the Mustard Seed and Leavened Bread
Matthew 13:31-35

Why is the *word of the kingdom* rarely taught in churches in the twenty-first century? And that includes churches from across the spectrum — liberal to fundamental. Why are those who teach the *word of the kingdom* criticized, ostracized, branded as heretics, and even persecuted? If the *word of the kingdom* is truth, then why do so few embrace it? Why do so many reject it? If these truths were taught at some point in the past, when did they fall by the wayside?

Jesus answers these questions in Matt. 13, in the parables of the mysteries of the kingdom. His answers are quite comforting and help to explain why so many refuse biblical teaching on the kingdom. Two thousand years ago Jesus predicted, using the medium of parables, how the *word of the kingdom* message would fare during the church age. Thus, we can make sense of the current state of things in Christianity by studying two more parables in Matt. 13 — 1) the parable of the mustard seed and, 2) the parable of the leavened bread. They explain the status quo.

The Kingdom of Heaven is Like …

Jesus starts out the parables in this chapter with the words: *The kingdom of heaven is like* (see vs. 24, 31, 33, 44, 45, 47, 52). In order to understand these parables correctly, we must again keep in mind the meaning of the term *kingdom of heaven* and how Christ uses it in these parables. As we discovered in previous chapters, the kingdom of heaven is not Heaven, per se. In other words, Jesus is not teaching about the gospel of grace, the gospel of salvation from eternal condemnation. The term *kingdom of heaven* is not about possessing eternal life and going to Heaven when you die. Unfortunately, that is what most evangelicals *think* it is referring to, but that is incorrect.

The kingdom of heaven literally translates *the kingdom of the heavens*, and it has to do with reward and ruling, not merely eternal existence. When John the Baptist and Jesus came on the scene, they began offering inclusion in the kingdom of the heavens to national Israel, if the nation would repent. According to Old Testament prophecy, Israel will inherit a position of rulership over the Gentile nations in the *earthly* Messianic kingdom. That is a given. Of course, some things need to happen before that promise is fulfilled, but that is one of the primary purposes of the tribulation — to bring national Israel to repentance. Nevertheless, at Christ's first coming He offered the nation something new that was only a mystery in the Old Testament. Jesus offered to Israel the privilege of ruling together with Him in the heavenly Jerusalem, the heavenly realm of the kingdom — the headquarters, if you will — and not merely in the earthly realm.

There are spiritual qualifications for being rewarded with an inheritance in the kingdom of the heavens, the ruling realm of the Messianic kingdom. Many in Israel — especially the religious leadership — did not see the need to repent of their sinful ways and stubbornly refused Christ's offer. Thus, Christ began speaking in parables, to reveal truth to those who were open-minded and teachable disciples, while concealing it from the close-minded who willfully chose to remain deaf and blind to truth.

All these things spake Jesus unto the multitude in parables; and without a parable spake he not unto them: That it might be

> fulfilled which was spoken by the prophet, saying, I will open my
> mouth in parables; I will utter things which have been kept secret
> from the foundation of the world. Matt. 13:34-35

After some time, sharing the gospel of the kingdom, Jesus
abruptly starts using parables in His teaching, which, as v. 35
reports, is in fulfillment of prophecy. This prophecy is found
in Psalm 78:2 and is quoted here in v. 35. Notice that the content of the parables had been hidden from before the foundation of the world. So this cannot be referring to salvation by
grace through faith alone. That was known throughout the
Old Testament and was never hidden as a secret or mystery.
The content of the parables is *the word of the kingdom*, as noted
previously in v. 19.

When Jesus uses the term, *the kingdom of heaven is like*, He is
using parables (metaphors in story form) to explain certain
aspects of the kingdom of heaven. In fact, His parables are
intended to answer the following questions:

1) What are the qualifications for inheriting the kingdom?
2) How will the good news of inheritance in the heavenly
   kingdom be received?
3) How will the word of the kingdom teaching fare in the
   present church age?
4) What will Satan do to oppose it and pervert it?
5) What will happen to those who reject it?
6) What will happen to those who accept it?

The Mustard Seed

> Another parable put he forth unto them, saying, The kingdom of
> heaven is like to a grain of mustard seed, which a man took, and
> sowed in his field: Which indeed is the least of all seeds: but when
> it is grown, it is the greatest among herbs, and becometh a tree, so
> that the birds of the air come and lodge in the branches thereof.
> Matt. 13:31-32

Mustard seeds are tiny, rather minuscule, but when
planted, they grow quickly. The kind of mustard plant that
Jesus has in mind is common in the Middle East. They are
evergreen shrubs that typically grow to about four feet in
height. Under the right conditions they can grow to heights of
fifteen to twenty feet. In that sense they can become a tree, of

sorts, at least compared with the average four-foot-high bush. However, the mustard "tree" is actually very "stemmy," more like a butterfly bush than an oak or pine.

The details about the tree are not critical. The point Jesus is making is that a tiny seed — about the size of the point of a ballpoint pen — grows into a large evergreen plant nearly twenty feet in height. That is what the kingdom of the heavens is like. In particular, that is how the word of the kingdom will fare, at least in the earliest stage of the church age.

From the tiny seed — the word of the kingdom preaching of John the Baptist and Jesus — the message spread quickly and came to characterize Christianity in the first century, the apostolic church. After Jesus and John, the message then spread to the twelve apostles, then to the seventy, then a few years later Paul took the message to the Gentile world, where it spread like wild fires. Despite starting out very small, the word of the kingdom spread rapidly and became a mighty tree of sorts. The first century apostolic church was well taught in the doctrine.

However, something ominous is introduced into this parable, giving us the impression that a dark cloud is hanging over the word of the kingdom doctrine, seeking to destroy it. What is the foreboding hint in the parable? The birds!

Those Ominous Birds

Many interpret this parable in a gospel sense, suggesting that as people get saved, the early church takes off and grows throughout the church age so that today it is mighty in size, its branches spreading throughout the entire earth. The fact that the birds of the air come to lodge in its branches suggests the blessing that the church of Jesus Christ is to all who find refuge there.

I believe that view is based on incorrect assumptions. For the context of these parables is not how the gospel of grace or even the church fares in the church age. The gospel of salvation from eternal condemnation is not the focus of these parables, nor is it the focus of the Synoptic Gospels. Rather, the word of the kingdom is in focus (again, I point you to v. 19, which is contextual).

Starting out ... mouth of Christ, ... and becomes like a ... interesting that Jesus ... sycamore tree, which are more hardy and ... ing from the ... rapidly, ... it is ... pines and oaks. Of course, there is a reason Jesus uses ... mustard tree imagery. Not only does it grow quickly, but the stemmy, overgrown evergreen bush, the mustard tree, is not going to remain strong for very long. It will be overcome, as we shall see. So Christ's imagery is highly appropriate, as we would expect.

The birds clearly represent the working of Satan. It would be inconsistent for the birds in the parable of the soils to represent the evil one eating up the seeds of the word of the kingdom that are sown on the wayside, and then in this parable to portray them as something positive. That would be confusing. Actually, the birds are evil, picturing the evil one who seeks to destroy the word of the kingdom.

In the Middle East it is common to see birds perching in the branches of the mustard tree, eating the seeds out of the seed pods. What a picture! Satan wants to keep children of God from becoming fruit-bearing children (Gr. *huios* – mature sons) of the kingdom. His plan is foiled when saints embrace the word of the kingdom message. When that happens, he resorts to Plan B, seeking to stop children of the kingdom from progressing in sanctification and bearing fruit so they will become disqualified from inheriting the kingdom.

Thus, the parable of the mustard seed illustrates how the word of the kingdom would be widely taught and widely received in the early church, like a quick-growing mustard tree. But then Satan would come along to destroy this work of God, making it ineffective. That leads us to the next parable which shows the effect of the birds.

The Leavened Bread

> Another parable spake he unto them; The kingdom of heaven is like unto leaven, which a woman took, and hid in three measures of meal, till the whole was leavened. Matt. 13:33

In commentaries on this passage, you will typically find

...one school of commentators sees ...ad as something positive. For example, ...or says it represents the working of the gospel ...art of a saved person so that saints are made com- ...etely new creatures. Another commentator says the leaven illustrates the spread of the church and its effectiveness over time in spreading truth in this present age. In fact, some Reformed commentators take this so far as to suggest the church will take over the world and will usher in a golden age. This view fits a-millennialism and post-millennialism quite well. But even some pre-millennial dispensationalists hold to this school, claiming that the leaven describes the advance of righteousness in the actual thousand year kingdom, not in the present age. So we have a school that views the leaven as having a positive effect.

The other school claims leaven is always used in the Scriptures as a type of corruption. The parable must, therefore, be speaking of the pervasiveness of leaven within the church, the leaven representing unbelievers who profess salvation but are actually unsaved counterfeits (like the tares, they say). While the latter view is closer to the correct interpretation, I believe it is incorrect, nonetheless.

Leaven, of course, is what we call yeast, a substance added to bread that pervades the whole loaf, causing it to ferment and rise. Leaven is always used in the Old Testament Scriptures to typify corruption. Leaven could never be used in the sacrificial offerings. Even in the New Testament Jesus said, *Beware of the leaven of the Pharisees and of the Sadducees*, Matt. 16:6.

Leaven is False Doctrine

There is no doubt in the minds of Jesus' audience as to what the leaven represents in the bread. Leaven is false doctrine. Jesus says the kingdom of heaven is like a woman baking bread. She takes three measures of grain, kneads it, and folds leaven into the loaf, setting it aside to pervade the entire lump. A little leaven leavens the whole lump (1 Cor. 5:6). On the heels of the two previous parables, the leaven can only have a destructive purpose.

In the parable of the wheat and tares, we find Satan inject-ing a counterfeit message alongside the word of the kingdom. The tares are those Christian leaders who have been unwit-tingly blinded by Satan to embrace and teach the counterfeit message — by downplaying the doctrine of eternal rewards, claiming all saints are overcomers, etc. In the parable of the mustard seed, we see Satan lodging in the branches of the mustard tree, ready to wreak havoc and destruction on the success of the word of the kingdom in the early church. Is he successful? Oh yes, terribly so! The counterfeit message in-jected by the tares, here represented by the leaven, is for the purpose of stopping the effectiveness of the word of the kingdom message and stopping children of the kingdom from bearing fruit, as the end of v. 33 says, *till the whole was leavened.*

Satan's Destruction of the Word of the Kingdom

This has been the result of Satan's working throughout the church age. We are now living in the day when the whole loaf has been leavened. Where is the word of the kingdom being taught today? Can you name five churches where these truths are taught? Can you name five pastors or Bible teachers that hold to these truths? But you can undoubtedly list hundreds of churches, even thousands, that *don't* believe or teach the word of the kingdom, if you use a directory or phone book.

What a tragedy, yet Jesus predicted this would happen by the end of the age. From the early church, taking off like a mustard tree, to the end of the age, the Laodicean church era — wretched and miserable and poor and blind and naked — completely leavened! The church of Jesus Christ is anemic.

Oh yes, there are many holding to fundamental Bible doctrines, but there are virtually none holding to the word of the kingdom. Yet, ironically, the word of the kingdom is the doctrine that presents the grand purpose and climax of Scripture. It is the doctrine that comprises virtually all of New Testament teaching, for it touches directly on matters of sanc-tification and Christian living.

It makes no difference whether a church is more liberal or conservative, word of the kingdom teaching is not found in either realm. Ironically, in Jesus' day, neither the Sadducees, who were the liberals of the day, nor the Pharisees, who were the legalistic fundamentalists, would have anything to do with Christ's kingdom offer. They both rejected it, even though they were worlds apart in their theology. And the same is true today!

While this ought to break our hearts, on the one hand, it is comforting on the other, to know we're not out on a theological limb of our own devising. We are believing and teaching and embracing truth, the same word of the kingdom truth that was taught by Jesus and the disciples in the first century, as characterized by the rapid mustard-tree-like growth.

How Did It Happen?

Then Satan flew into the tree. A casual reading of Acts 20:17-32 reveals that the insidious working of Satan to destroy the word of the kingdom message had already begun near the end of the apostle Paul's ministry. By the second century there were more compromises, and by the time of Constantine the church was partnering with the world and leaving off the message of the kingdom. Then came the dark ages of the church, when truth was veiled and plunged into spiritual darkness. Only after many centuries of deception and lies was the gospel of salvation by faith alone rescued in the Reformation. But Satan ensured that coming out of the Reformation, the doctrine of sanctification would be muddled, tied together with justification in the Calvinist teaching of Perseverance. In so doing Satan put a stranglehold, a death-grip, on word of the kingdom teaching.

That is the state in which we find ourselves today. Hardly anyone believes that saints must qualify to inherit the kingdom of the heavens. Virtually no one believes that children of God must bear fruit by the grace of God if they expect to rule together with Jesus. Virtually no one believes in the possibility of negative reward at the Judgment Seat. As a result, the love of many has waxed cold, and the church is more licentious than ever. The downward spiral is mapped out quite clearly in the letters to the seven churches in Rev. 2-3.

Throughout the centuries, Satan has so counterfeited and perverted the message to the point that the entire church of

Jesus Christ is now poisoned with respect to the word of the kingdom. The leaven has pervaded the whole.

It should comfort us to know that Jesus predicted this would happen. So don't lose heart! Keep believing and teaching the word of the kingdom, living faithfully unto the Lord, and you will inherit the kingdom! To that end, Christ makes you an offer:

> Behold, I stand at the door, and knock: if any man hear my voice, and open the door, I will come in to him, and will sup with him, and he with me. To him that overcometh will I grant to sit with me in my throne, even as I also overcame, and am set down with my Father in his throne. He that hath an ear, let him hear what the Spirit saith unto the churches. Rev. 3:20-22

Will you listen to the Spirit of God? Will you open the door to Christ, and let Him come in to fellowship with you?

Chapter 4

Treasures Old and New

Parables of the Hidden Treasure, the Pearl, the Net
Matthew 13:44-52

A Brief Review of the First Four Parables

Thus far we have studied four parables that Jesus refers to as "the mysteries of the kingdom of heaven." First, in the parable of the four soils, we see four responses to the word of the kingdom message. Some reject it entirely. Some receive it ambitiously, but then cower in fear and abandon the word of the kingdom when pressured or persecuted. Some receive it ambitiously, then fizzle later when lured by worldly things. In other words, they don't live it. Finally, some receive it with joy and live it, bearing fruit in some quantity. Those in the final group that embrace the word of the kingdom and bear fruit become the center of Satan's attacks.

Second, in the parable of the wheat and tares, we learn that Satan attempts to stop them from bearing fruit and from spreading the message of the kingdom by planting tares alongside as counterfeits. The tares are not unbelievers. Rather, they are Christian leaders (preachers and teachers) who proclaim a counterfeit message. How? By diluting the doctrine of eternal rewards, and by teaching saints they are all overcomers and will all rule with Jesus, and by gospelizing the Synoptic Gospels. In so doing, they are implicitly condoning licentious living, and they are hindering saints from seeing the seriousness of preparing to inherit the kingdom. The counterfeit message of the tares sounds similar to the word of the kingdom, but with a strange twist.

Third, the parable of the mustard tree tells of a tiny mustard seed growing very quickly into a tree or large bush. This undoubtedly refers to the immediate growth of the word of the kingdom message in the first century early church. But that all changes very rapidly, for the birds perch in the tree, pointing to something ominous.

Fourth, the parable of the leaven explains what happens to thwart the early success of the word of the kingdom. Satan inserts leaven — the counterfeit teaching of the tares — into the word of the kingdom message. Over time the error pervades the entire message, thereby corrupting it. Indeed, this explains why in our era hardly anyone believes or teaches the word of the kingdom. It also explains why the church of Jesus Christ is anemic, like the Laodicean church, wretched and miserable and poor and blind and naked.

These first four parables describe how the word of the kingdom message will fare up to the end of the church age. But the next three parables are a bit different. In fact, before Jesus shares these last three parables, there is a change of audience and even teaching venue.

> Then Jesus sent the multitude away, and went into the house: and his disciples came unto him. Matt. 13:36a

Jesus is no longer addressing the multitudes. Now He is speaking only to His closest disciples. He gives them three more parables that take the first four beyond the church age, into the tribulation and up to the return of Christ. It could be that Christ dismisses the multitude because these parables are even more difficult to grasp. Perhaps the broader audience is not mature enough to receive these final parables.

Parable of the Hidden Treasure

> Again, the kingdom of heaven is like unto treasure hid in a field;

the which when a man hath found, he hideth, and for joy thereof goeth and selleth all that he hath, and buyeth that field. Matt. 13:44

Jesus does not give the interpretation, so we are on our own. Thankfully, there are some hints in the text, and we have the added advantage of the completed revelation of Scripture. From v. 38 (discussed in Ch. 2), we know the meaning of the field. *The field is the world*, that is, the inhabited earth. It is not Israel, nor is it the church. It is the earth. What, then, is the treasure hidden in the earth? We can answer this question from other Scripture passages.

For the LORD hath chosen Jacob unto himself, and Israel for his peculiar treasure. Psalm 135:4

Now therefore, if ye will obey my voice indeed, and keep my covenant, then ye shall be a peculiar treasure unto me above all people: for all the earth is mine: And ye shall be unto me a kingdom of priests, and an holy nation. Exod. 19:5-6a

According to these passages, who is God's treasure? Israel is God's treasure, and the field is the earth. Interestingly, in the parable the man does not purchase Israel, the treasure. He purchases the field. Hold that thought; we will get back to it, for it is important.

Who is the man? I believe it is Jesus Christ, and that will become clearer as we go along. In what sense does the man, Jesus, find the treasure and then hide it? When Jesus came to Earth the first time, He was born into a Jewish family, having royal lineage, extending back to King David. In that sense He "found" Israel, the treasure. In fact, once His public ministry began, Jesus focused His message on the nation, God's treasure.

Take another look at Exod. 19:5 above. It is a conditional promise: *If* ye will obey. Of course, Israel did not obey. Thus, Christ's public ministry to His people the Jews was about calling them back to obedience. The message He preached was for this express purpose. *Repent, for the kingdom of heaven is at hand*, Matt. 4:17. To paraphrase, "Get right with God, and you will once again be His peculiar treasure, you will be a kingdom of priests — priest-kings, in fact — and a holy nation."

The Kingdom of the Heavens Rejected by Israel

Jesus offered Israel the privilege of ruling together with Him in the heavenly ruling realm of the kingdom. But Israel rejected the offer! The religious leaders who represented the nation had the attitude: *We have Abraham to our father*. In other words, "As children of Abraham, we are spiritually qualified to inherit the kingdom." It was an arrogant and self-sufficient attitude. In fact, their rejection of Christ's offer got so intense that they committed the unpardonable sin.

> Then the Pharisees went out, and held a council against him, how they might destroy him. Matt. 12:14

How remarkable! His "treasure" didn't hear Him out. Instead, they sought to destroy Him. Then Jesus healed a man and cast the demons out of him. The response of the audience was mixed.

> And all the people were amazed, and said, Is not this the son of David? But when the Pharisees heard it, they said, This fellow doth not cast out devils, but by Beelzebub the prince of the devils. Matt. 12:23-24

The Pharisees condemned Jesus, claiming that He cast out the demons in the power of Satan. This is the unpardonable sin that consigned the nation to Judgment.

> He that is not with me is against me; and he that gathereth not with me scattereth abroad. Wherefore I say unto you, All manner of sin and blasphemy shall be forgiven unto men: but the blasphemy against the Holy Ghost shall not be forgiven unto men. And whosoever speaketh a word against the Son of man, it shall be forgiven him: but whosoever speaketh against the Holy Ghost, it shall not be forgiven him, neither in this world, neither in the world to come. Either make the tree good, and his fruit good; or else make the tree corrupt, and his fruit corrupt: for the tree is known by his fruit. O generation of vipers, how can ye, being evil, speak good things? for out of the abundance of the heart the mouth speaketh. A good man out of the good treasure of the heart bringeth forth good things: and an evil man out of the evil treasure bringeth forth evil things. But I say unto you, That every idle word that men shall speak, they shall give account thereof in the day of judgment. For by thy words thou shalt be justified, and by thy words thou shalt be condemned. Matt. 12:30-37

On the heels of this indictment, the Pharisees had the gall to ask Him for another sign, even after He had performed several miracles. Do you see what happened in Matt. 12? The religious leadership refused to recognize Jesus as the Son of God. They ignored the signs (miracles), asking for yet more signs (v. 38). They rejected the offer of the kingdom of the heavens, on the basis that Abraham was their father (Matt. 3:9). Matt. 12 is the point at which the religious leadership sealed the nation's destiny. Look where it leads.

> Therefore say I unto you, The kingdom of God shall be taken from you, and given to a nation bringing forth the fruits thereof. Matt. 21:43

The Kingdom Given to the Church

We understand the "other nation" to be the church. Now we can make sense of our parable.

> Again, the kingdom of heaven is like unto treasure hid in a field; the which when a man hath found, he hideth, and for joy thereof goeth and selleth all that he hath, and buyeth that field. Matt. 13:44

The man is Jesus. The treasure is Israel. The fact that Jesus hides the treasure signifies His taking away the heavenly kingdom from the nation of Israel and giving it to the church. Essentially, Israel goes into "hiding" in the church age. Ah, but that's not the end. The man Jesus is going to purchase the field. How will He purchase the field? By selling all He has. This is undoubtedly a reference to His death on the cross — His great redemption — wherein He gave everything to pay the price. However, notice that He doesn't purchase the *treasure* by His death; He purchases the *field* (the earth).

How do we make sense of this? The answer is found in the book of Revelation.

> And I saw in the right hand of him that sat on the throne a book written within and on the backside, sealed with seven seals. And no man in heaven, nor in earth, neither under the earth, was able to open the book, neither to look thereon. Rev. 5:1, 3

God the Father is on His throne, holding in His right hand a scroll with seven seals, but no one is qualified to open it.

John starts weeping, for this implies we cannot know the future. One of the elders tells him not to weep, for the Lion of the tribe of Judah is worthy to take the scroll and open it. John looks and sees in the midst of the throne, not a lion, but *a lamb as it had been slain* — an obvious reference to Jesus, post-crucifixion — after paying the price to purchase the field. But He has not yet received the title deed to Earth. He will accomplish that in the tribulation. The sealed scroll is the title deed to Earth. By opening the scroll, Jesus will bring judgment upon the earth and upon antichrist and His Gentile forces, but most importantly upon Israel for the purpose of bringing the nation back to repentance.

Why is Jesus worthy to redeem the earth?

> And they sung a new song, saying, Thou art worthy to take the book, and to open the seals thereof: for thou wast slain, and hast redeemed us to God by thy blood out of every kindred, and tongue, and people, and nation; And hast made us unto our God kings and priests: and we shall reign on the earth. Rev. 5:9-10

He earned the right by paying the price at His crucifixion. We know from Old Testament prophecy that when He returns the second time, He will forever defeat Satan, taking crowns away from the evil one. Jesus will then give those crowns to His faithful, fruitful saints, the ones He deems worthy at His Judgment Seat. They will rule together with Him in the heavenly realm over the earth in the millennium. But that only applies to the church.

National Israel Restored

What about Israel? Because she rejected the offer of ruling in the heavenly kingdom at Christ's first coming, the nation will be consigned to ruling on Earth, the very Earth that Jesus purchases back from Satan by His blood. Then Israel will once again be restored as the wife of Jehovah and will rule on the earth over the nations of the world. Something must happen before this restoration can occur.

> And this gospel of the kingdom shall be preached in all the world for a witness unto all nations; and then shall the end come. Matt. 24:14

The 144,000 Jewish evangelists will go around the world, pointing the Jews to salvation in Jesus (and Gentiles as well). They will also preach another message — the gospel of the kingdom — the message that repentance is required before the nation can be restored. Does the nation repent and become restored? Oh yes! Zechariah says, *They shall look upon me whom they have pierced, and they shall mourn for him, as one mourneth for his only son, and shall be in bitterness for him, as one that is in bitterness for his firstborn,* Zech. 12:10. Israel will not only believe on Jesus as the Son of God, she will also repent of her past failure and turn to the Lord. Thus, the parable of the treasure is about Jesus hiding Israel at His first coming and paying the price to redeem the earth, then at His second coming retaking the earth and reclaiming His treasure, giving Israel rule over the millennial Earth. What a plan! It's all summarized in this little parable of just one verse.

Parable of the Pearl of Great Price

> Again, the kingdom of heaven is like unto a merchant man, seeking goodly pearls: Who, when he had found one pearl of great price, went and sold all that he had, and bought it. Matt. 13:45-46

The man in this parable is obviously the same as the man in the previous parable, Jesus Christ. Selling all He has signifies His redemptive death on the cross. In both parables (this one and the previous) something happens *after* Christ's redemption on Calvary, not concurrent with it. In the parable of the hidden treasure, the purchase takes place chronologically much later, in the tribulation, when Jesus redeems the earth on the basis of His redemptive work on Calvary. Here, the purchase is also chronologically later, long after His finished work on Calvary.

What is this one pearl of great price that Christ purchases after He has paid the redemptive price, but on the basis of His redemption? As we shall see, He purchases the *pearl* at the same time He purchases the *field*. But rather than Israel being the focus of this parable, as in the previous one, the *church* is in focus.

Pearls are the product of shellfish, oysters in particular, which were considered unclean in the dietary restrictions under the Mosaic Law. Furthermore, pearls are found in the sea, which symbolizes Gentile nations in the Bible. Thus the pearl would be an inappropriate image to describe the nation of Israel, but it would be apropos as symbolizing the Church. More specifically, the pearl represents the bride of Christ, the subset of the church that is found faithful at the Judgment Seat.

How can we arrive at this conclusion about the pearl? We must remember that these parables are not about the gospel and the matter of saved people being given eternal life. They are about the word of the kingdom and how saints will respond to it. It would be inconsistent with the sequence of parables in this chapter if the pearl were to represent all saints, regardless of obedience and fruitfulness. No, in the context, the pearl of great price must represent those faithful, fruit-bearing saints found worthy at the Judgment Seat who will become Christ's bride and co-regent. They are the sons unto glory, the mature firstborn inheritors of the kingdom of the heavens.

Parable of the Fishing Net

> 47 Again, the kingdom of heaven is like unto a net, that was cast into the sea, and gathered of every kind:
> 48 Which, when it was full, they drew to shore, and sat down, and gathered the good into vessels, but cast the bad away.
> 49 So shall it be at the end of the world: the angels shall come forth, and sever the wicked from among the just,
> 50 And shall cast them into the furnace of fire: there shall be wailing and gnashing of teeth. Matt. 13:47-50

Like the previous parable, this one also takes matters out to the very end of the age. Again, we must keep in mind that the kingdom of the heavens is in view, as v. 47 indicates. Specifically, it is the proffered kingdom and the response to the offer.

As we saw in the parables of the hidden treasure and the pearl of great price, Jesus first offered the kingdom of the heavens to Israel, but when Israel rejected it, Jesus took it from that nation and gave it to the church. In the parable of the fishing net, we find the response of the church to the same kingdom offer.

The net is a fishing net that is thrown into the sea. It is dragged along for some time in the sea, then hauled in to shore to sort the catch. In the Scriptures, the sea represents Gentile nations. Thus, the fish in the net represent the saved of the church age, predominantly Gentiles. They are now part of the church, an entity distinct from Israel and from the Gentile world.

However, the focus of the parable is not on the catching, but on the sorting, so the emphasis is not on salvation, per se, but on responses to Christ's kingdom offer. Indeed, as stated earlier, all seven mysteries of the kingdom parables in Matt. 13 have to do with the word of the kingdom, not matters of eternal salvation from Hell.

Notice at the end of v. 47, there are *gathered of every kind*. This is likely a reference to the parable of the four soils at the beginning of this chapter, which represents four types of responses to the kingdom of the heavens offer. According to v. 48, the catch is sorted into *good* and *bad*. This is in keeping with the words of the apostle Paul.

> For we must all appear before the judgment seat of Christ; that every one may receive the things done in his body, according to that he hath done, whether it be good or bad. 2 Cor. 5:10

The *good* in Matt. 13:48 are the *just* in v. 49 — a word that means righteous, those who live uprightly. Since all in the net are saved, the word *just* cannot be referring to positional or imputed righteousness. It must, in context, be referring to practical righteousness, what we might call righteous behavior. These are fruit-bearing saints. The *bad* in v. 48 are the *wicked* in v. 49, a word that means lawless. Their behavior as saints has not been righteous; it has been licentious. These are carnal saints that do not take the kingdom offer of Jesus seriously.

According to v. 49, the angels will come at the end of the world (*age*) to sever (*separate*) these saved people of the church into two categories — good and bad — righteous and licentious. In like manner as the parable of the wheat and tares, this judgment happens simultaneously for good and bad. That means the good and bad cannot be referring to saved and lost because the Scriptures are very clear that lost folks are judged *after* the millennium (Rev. 20:11-15), which is one thousand years after this sorting out. Even these "bad" ones are saved people. But they are cast away (*out*), v. 48. This is undoubtedly a reference to the outer darkness — the relative darkness outside Christ's bright heavenly ruling realm. The darkness outside is the earthly realm of the kingdom. For more on outer darkness, see Chapters 9 and 12 in this book and also Chapter 10 in my book, *The End of the Pilgrimage.*

The reference to being cast into the furnace of fire troubles some students of the Word because they assume it is Hell. However, it is not a reference to Hell (i.e., the lake of fire). It is a reference to the Judgment Seat fires, as in the parable of the wheat and tares. <u>For a wicked saint to be cast into the furnace of fire is a metaphor for a Christian's works being burned up at the Judgment Seat, and consequently the saint loses rewards and is cast into the darkness outside</u>. Don't let the term *furnace of fire* deter you from interpreting this parable correctly. The bottom line is that after the fiery Bema these saved folks are left outside the New Jerusalem and are not given the opportunity to dwell with Christ and rule with Him in the millennial kingdom. Why? Because they rejected His kingdom offer to repent of their sins and bear fruit for the glory of the Lord. When they receive their verdict at the Bema, they will regret it, wailing and gnashing their teeth, which is the oriental way of expressing grief and sorrow — crying loudly and gritting the teeth in regret.

Old and New Treasures

Jesus closes this chapter and the seven parables describing the mysteries of the kingdom, with v. 52.

> Then said he unto them, Therefore every scribe which is instructed unto the kingdom of heaven is like unto a man that is an householder, which bringeth forth out of his treasure things new and old. Matt. 13:52

Those who are teachable and learn the word of the kingdom are like a householder who can bring out of his storeroom old treasures and even new treasures. What are things old and new, according to the context here? The old things are truths that have already been understood and embraced by the student of the Word, doctrines he or she has known for years. The new things are truths that were not previously known or understood. The student is learning something fresh and new and vibrant from the Scriptures. The Word of God is like a mine, containing gems and nuggets that can be yours if you will do the seeking and digging.

Those who are not open to word of the kingdom teaching, who refuse or resist it, live in a box, and the box is all they know. Their storeroom does not have old and new treasures, only old ones. They are narrow in their thinking and resistant to something new from God's Word. Incidentally, truth is not new; it has been around as long as the Word of God has existed. But we don't always see it. I believe this verse is teaching that those who receive word of the kingdom teaching will always be finding new, fresh truths from God's Word that they had not seen before.

Understanding the word of the kingdom is the hermeneutical *key* to understanding the whole Bible. No wonder Satan is working so hard to keep children of God blinded from this truth, to keep them from becoming sons unto glory.

Chapter 5

Inheriting Eternal Life

Parable of the Good Samaritan
Luke 10:25-37

The Typical Forced Interpretation

A lawyer comes to Jesus with a question: *Master, what shall I do to inherit eternal life?* Luke 10:25. That question and Christ's answer have been misinterpreted repeatedly by those who tend to "gospelize" much of the New Testament, especially the parables. The lawyer is not asking how to receive the gift of eternal life so he can go to Heaven when he dies. If he were asking that question, then Christ's answer would be a convolution of the gospel of grace by faith alone. For Jesus essentially tells the man to obey the Mosaic Law, and he will live (v. 28). Of course, Jesus would never muddy the waters on truth. He obviously knows that salvation is by grace through faith alone, not of works. He would never tell someone to work for their salvation.

I am amazed at the interpretive gymnastics that many commentators employ to try to explain the parable of the Good Samaritan as a salvation text without making it sound as if salvation is by works. Frankly, it can't be done unless assumptions are made that are inconsistent with the text. The assumptions are forced on the passage, based on one's theological paradigm.

For instance, one common explanation is that the lawyer is justifying his salvation based on his obedience to the law. So Jesus shows him through the parable that he cannot keep the law of himself. What he needs is Christ's righteousness. Those who try to explain the parable in this way typically say that Jesus is the Good Samaritan. But that still doesn't explain why Jesus says to the lawyer in v. 37, *Go and do likewise*, as if to suggest that if the man becomes benevolent like Jesus, then he will be saved. That is *not* what Jesus is teaching. Rather, those who cannot imagine Jesus is talking to a believer about inheriting the kingdom force it upon the passage.

The Correct Meaning of Inheriting Eternal Life

How do we rightly divide this parable? How do we make sense of this man's question and Christ's answer? What you will rarely, if ever, hear from the pulpit or in commentaries, is the correct meaning of *inheriting eternal life*. Most interpret the phrase to mean "getting saved and thereby receiving a ticket to Heaven." But that is not what the phrase means.

Whenever we see the phrase *eternal life* in the New Testament, we must determine according to context, is it referring to the *gift* of eternal life — salvation by faith alone — or to the *reward* of eternal life, which is eternal *reward* according to works? They are two different aspects or degrees of eternal life. A classic example of the *reward* of eternal life is found in the book of Galatians:

> Be not deceived; God is not mocked: for whatsoever a man soweth, that shall he also reap. For he that soweth to his flesh shall of the flesh reap corruption; but he that soweth to the Spirit shall of the Spirit reap life everlasting. Gal. 6:7-8

Reaping *life everlasting*, in this context, is the result of works — when a believer sows to the Spirit rather than the flesh, and sowing involves doing. It cannot be referring to the *gift* of eternal life, which is according to faith alone. It is referring to the *reward* of eternal life, which is according to works. Thus, in the context of Luke 10, the lawyer is asking Jesus, not how he can be saved and merely possess endless life, but how he can inherit the reward of eternal life that results in ruling in the kingdom. The same is true with respect to the rich young ruler texts in Matt. 19, Mark 10, and Luke 18.

Amongst those who arrive at this correct interpretation of *inheriting eternal life* are two groups of theologians that take entirely different approaches for arriving at their conclusions. A full discussion of the two positions is outside the scope of this book, but a brief overview will be given below.

Group #1: Rewards Are Eternal

Some theologians[1] believe that ultimate recompense for believers — whether positive or negative — will have eternal consequence and will not be limited merely to the Messianic kingdom age. They base their position, in part, on the following Old Testament text:

> And many of them that sleep in the dust of the earth shall awake, some to everlasting life, and some to shame *and* everlasting contempt. And they that be wise shall shine as the brightness of the firmament; and they that turn many to righteousness as the stars for ever and ever. Daniel 12:2-3

The lawyer (also the rich young ruler) would have known of this Old Testament teaching. Thus, by asking Jesus, *Master, what shall I do to inherit eternal life?* he would have been inquiring as to how he could have eternal reward in the everlasting kingdom. He desired to shine forever.

Group #2: Rewards Are Limited to the Messianic Age

Other theologians[2] believe that rewards (positive and negative) are limited to the Messianic kingdom age. This position is based on understanding the Greek adjective *aionios*, typically translated *eternal* in the New Testament, as actually meaning "age-enduring."[3] Context must be considered to determine whether the age-enduring life is eternal in scope (e.g., John 3:16) or merely limited to the Messianic kingdom age. The lawyer, they say, was asking how he could be rewarded and rule with Jesus in His Messianic kingdom.

Not Eternal Salvation, But Inheritance in the Kingdom

Either way, whether rewards are eternal or limited to the Messianic age alone, the request of this lawyer has nothing to do with eternal salvation from condemnation, the doctrine of soteriology. He is asking about inheritance in the kingdom, the doctrine of rewards — referred to by some as *misthology*.[4]

This man wants to rule with Jesus, but he's skeptical of the requirements. He probably thinks, like the Pharisees, that he's a "shoo-in" because of his national heritage. That is why he is tempting (testing) Jesus. Some suggest that this indicates he is unsaved. But do not saved people test the Lord? Did not Israel test God after they left Egypt as redeemed people? Indeed, they tempted God numerous times. The point is that this man is not inquiring as to how to be saved from Hell. Presumably, he is already saved. Jesus never talks with this man about matters of salvation. Rather, Jesus tells him how to qualify to inherit the ruling realm of the kingdom, the kingdom of the heavens, the heavenly New Jerusalem. According to this text, what is the qualification?

> He said unto him, What is written in the law? how readest thou? And he answering said, Thou shalt love the Lord thy God with all thy heart, and with all thy soul, and with all thy strength, and with all thy mind; and thy neighbour as thyself. And he said unto him, Thou hast answered right: this do, and thou shalt live. Luke 10:26-28

If this man is asking about salvation, then Jesus is giving him a works-salvation answer. But that most certainly is not the case. If anyone knows the way to Heaven, Jesus does. He also knows what this man is asking. The man does not want to know how to get to Heaven but how to inherit the kingdom of the heavens. Keep in mind that just because you are a child of God, doesn't mean you will be given the privilege of ruling with Him.

Esau, the eldest son of Isaac, was passed over because he cared not for spiritual things. Jacob was given the birthright of the firstborn instead. Reuben, the eldest son of Jacob, was passed over and did not receive the inheritance of the first-born because he took his father's concubine. The inheritance was given to Joseph instead. Even Israel as a nation, God's firstborn, forfeited the inheritance of the Promised Land because they did not believe God but believed the spies instead. As a result, they could not enter but died in the wilderness. Another generation entered instead.

Inheritance Is Earned by Loving Your Neighbor

The same could apply to you. You are not a "shoo-in" for the heavenly kingdom of reward, just because you are a child of God. You must earn the privilege, and the qualification is summed up in v. 27 above. Do you love the Lord your God with all your heart and soul and strength and mind? Do you love your neighbor as yourself? If you do this, you will *live*. Moses had said to the people in Lev. 18:5, *Ye shall therefore keep my statutes, and my judgments: which if a man do, he shall live in them: I am the LORD*. There is *life* in obeying the Lord — vibrancy of communion and fellowship.

Are you fulfilling the moral law of God, as expressed in the Ten Commandments and summed up in these two? This is the law of Christ. Incidentally, dear Christian, you have the provision to do so. The provision is Jesus, who lives within you through His Holy Spirit. Rom. 8:4 says, *That the righteousness of the law might be fulfilled in us, who walk not after the flesh, but after the Spirit*. You can obey the law of Christ in the power of the Holy Spirit, but that is the only way you can do so. You cannot of yourself. Incidentally, if you are obeying the law of Christ, then you are truly living, here and now.

Perhaps you are like this lawyer who, *willing to justify himself, said unto Jesus, And who is my neighbour?* Luke 10:29. You're thinking, "I'm saved, I'm a child of God, so I'm an automatic heir of the kingdom of the heavens." That is not correct. Maybe, like this lawyer, you think you're obeying the law of Christ, generally speaking. But you want to know how far this matter of loving your neighbor goes. What does God mean when He says to love your neighbor as yourself? The answer is found in this parable of the Good Samaritan.

An Unlikely Neighbor

And Jesus answering said, A certain man went down from Jerusalem to Jericho, and fell among thieves, which stripped him of his raiment, and wounded him, and departed, leaving him half dead. And by chance there came down a certain priest that way: and when he saw him, he passed by on the other side. And likewise a Levite, when he was at the place, came and looked on him, and passed by on the other side. Luke 10:30-32

A presumably Jewish man travels alone from Jerusalem down to Jericho. <u>The city of Jericho is actually northeast of Jerusalem, but you always go down when leaving Jerusalem.</u> The trip, one-way on foot, is about eighteen miles, and it's all downhill, a drop of about three thousand feet. The terrain can be treacherous for traveling, not just because of the Judean wilderness, but also because of the thieves that hide in the mountains. Indeed, this poor man gets mugged by thieves, and they not only take all of his possessions, including his clothing, they also beat him so badly that he is half-dead. Apparently, the man is lying alongside the road, undoubtedly bleeding, maybe even internally. He is in bad shape.

A priest comes along on the road but avoids the man, passing by on the other side. Then a Levite comes down the road. He is not a priest, per se, but is also engaged in temple service in some capacity. He also avoids the man and crosses over to the other side of the road. We are told clearly that both men see the left-for-dead traveler. Why don't they stop? We don't know, but maybe they consider it inconvenient. Or perhaps they fear the man could be dead, and they don't want to become unclean by touching him.

This is legalism! For they are putting the intricacies of the ceremonial law — and their burdensome interpretation of it — above the moral law, helping others. Doesn't that often happen in modern Christian churches? Some get so caught up with the intricacies of their separational position — those matters of application, such as music standards, dress standards, hair standards, philosophy of ministry, etc. — and they equate those matters of application with doctrine. They live for their applications, even to the point of hurting people and causing spiritual casualties. They have the attitude, "We are right and others are wrong," and they separate from everyone else. They consider it a badge of honor to fight with those who are not like them — shooting at others, even the wounded in their midst who don't understand.

How is this any different than crossing on the other side of the road and refusing to help the wounded traveller? Every twenty-first century church needs to ask, "Master, what must we do to inherit eternal life? What changes are necessary, Lord, if we would rule with you in the age to come?" It could be that many churches and saints of God desperately need to heed the parable of the Good Samaritan. Do you love others as yourself? The parable continues in vs. 33-35:

> But a certain Samaritan, as he journeyed, came where he was: and when he saw him, he had compassion on him, and went to him, and bound up his wounds, pouring in oil and wine, and set him on his own beast, and brought him to an inn, and took care of him. And on the morrow when he departed, he took out two pence, and gave them to the host, and said unto him, Take care of him; and whatsoever thou spendest more, when I come again, I will repay thee. Luke 10:33-35

Put Aside Prejudices and Differences

It is important to remember that the Jews and Samaritans of Christ's day had hostilities toward each other, not unlike the hatred and hostility some Christians have for others unlike them. The disdain, the contempt, the condescension has to go! This Samaritan puts aside nationalistic prejudices and takes the time to minister to this hurting Jewish man. The Samaritan dresses his wounds and then puts the man on his donkey, taking him to an inn, where he can rest and find further care. In fact, the Samaritan goes so far as to pay two pence (two days' wages) toward the man's hotel bill. If more is owed because the man needs a longer convalescent time, then the Samaritan will pay when he returns.

The actions of the Good Samaritan are Christ-like. Indeed, this is the loving heart and character of our Lord. In the parable the Good Samaritan represents any New Testament church age believer who demonstrates love for others by ministering to their needs. Those who love in this manner will inherit eternal life.

> Then shall the King say unto them on his right hand, Come, ye blessed of my Father, inherit the kingdom prepared for you from the foundation of the world: For I was an hungred, and ye gave me meat: I was thirsty, and ye gave me drink: I was a stranger, and ye

took me in: Naked, and ye clothed me: I was sick, and ye visited me: I was in prison, and ye came unto me. Matt. 25:34-36

This lawyer thinks he is pretty good, until Jesus tells him the story of the good Samaritan. In the end, after sharing the parable, Jesus asks the lawyer, *Which now of these three, thinkest thou, was neighbour unto him that fell among the thieves?* Luke 10:36. Without hesitation, the lawyer replies, *He that shewed mercy on him,* v. 37. <u>Your neighbor is anyone God brings across your path and your duty is to treat that one with the mercy and compassion of the Lord</u>. As Jesus says to the lawyer, so He says to you, *Go, and do thou likewise,* v. 37.

There is clearly an application for you to reach out to people in need. But there is also an application that you not become caught up with the setting of legalistic standards that get in the way of right relationships with other people. Oh, that the church of Jesus Christ would wake up and see the need to be merciful to other churches and other saints and to those who are hurting! We need to weep o'er the erring one and lift up the fallen. Children of God, go and do likewise, and you will inherit the kingdom.

---

[1] For example, see Marty Cauley, *Rewards are Eternal: Rewards Cannot Be Limited to the Millennial Kingdom*, 2015.

[2] For example, see Arlen Chitwood, *The Time of the End: A Study About the Book of Revelation*, discussion of *aionios*, pp. 320-321. See also S.S. Craig, *The Dualism of Eternal Life.*

[3] Marvin R. Vincent, *Word Studies in the New Testament* (Peabody, MA: Hendrickson Publ., no copyright), vol. 4, 58-59.

[4] Term coined by Marty Cauley, based on the Greek word *misthos*, meaning "reward."

Chapter 6

Did the Rich Young Ruler Go to Hell?

Parable of the Entitled Workers
Matt. 19:30-20:16

While celebrating my son's fifth birthday many years ago, my wife announced that cake and ice cream was ready to be served. The birthday boy darted toward the table and blurted out, "Me first!" Disappointed with her son's blatant selfishness, my wife corrected him by quoting Scripture, "The first shall be last, and the last shall be first." Without missing a beat, our five-year-old said, "Then, me last!" He fully expected, of course, that he would be served first. He missed the point entirely.

In God's economy, things we take for granted are often turned upside-down. For instance, the humble are exalted, while the high and lofty are abased. Servants are promoted to chiefs, not those who vie for position. The first are made last and the last first. This reversal of roles is emphasized twice, as . bookends of sorts, hemming in the parable of the entitled workers (Matt. 20:1-16) that we will consider in this chapter.

Many that are first shall be last; and the last shall be first. Matt. 19:30

So the last shall be first, and the first last: for many be called, but few chosen. Matt. 20:16

The parable that will be examined later in this chapter is found between these verses and starts out, *For the kingdom of heaven is like*, Matt. 20:1. Once again we find a parable describing some aspect of the kingdom of the heavens. As we shall see, Jesus is giving one criterion by which He rewards at the Judgment Seat. But to fully understand this parable we must interpret it within context. The broader context goes all the way back to Matt. 19:16, the account of the rich young ruler.

16 And, behold, one came and said unto him, Good Master, what good thing shall I do, that I may have eternal life?
17 And he said unto him, Why callest thou me good? there is none good but one, that is, God: but if thou wilt enter into life, keep the commandments.
18 He saith unto him, Which? Jesus said, Thou shalt do no murder, Thou shalt not commit adultery, Thou shalt not steal, Thou shalt not bear false witness,
19 Honour thy father and thy mother: and, Thou shalt love thy neighbour as thyself.
20 The young man saith unto him, All these things have I kept from my youth up: what lack I yet?
21 Jesus said unto him, If thou wilt be perfect, go and sell that thou hast, and give to the poor, and thou shalt have treasure in heaven: and come and follow me.
22 But when the young man heard that saying, he went away sorrowful: for he had great possessions. Matt. 19:16-22

In the parallel account of this parable in Luke 18 the man is referred to as a ruler. Here in v. 22 he is simply called a "young man." Some commentators say this probably means he is the chief leader of a synagogue; others say he could be a member of the Sanhedrin. Either way, he is a man who knows the Mosaic Law.

There is a clear connection between Christ's encounter with the rich young ruler (19:16-30) and the parable of the entitled workers (20:1-16). For instance, in 19:16 the ruler asks, *Good Master, what good thing shall I do, that I may have eternal life?* Jesus responds, *Why callest thou me good? There is none good but one, that is, God*, v. 17. Compare that discussion of *good* with 20:15, *Is it not lawful for me to do what I will with mine own? Is thine eye evil, because I am good?* This is clearly a reference to the ruler and his way of thinking that characterizes the mentality of much of the Jewish leadership of Christ's day.

In order to fully understand the parable, we must first seek to understand the conversation between Jesus and the ruler, followed by the conversation between Jesus and His disciples. Guiding our exposition of this passage will be four simple points: 1. The ruler's question; 2. Christ's reply; 3. The disciples' questions; and 4. The parabolic conclusion.

1. The Ruler's Question

When the ruler asked, *Good Master, what good thing shall I do, that I may have eternal life?* what was he asking? The typical answer given by commentators across the evangelical spectrum is that the ruler wanted to know how to be saved from eternal condemnation and be given eternal life. They go on to say that Jesus pointed the ruler to the law to demonstrate to the man that he really could not keep the law in its entirety and therefore could not expect to be declared righteous by his good works. In other words, he could not have eternal life because he could not possibly keep the law. The ruler's unwillingness to sell his possessions and give to the poor demonstrates that he was covetous and in violation of the tenth commandment, thou shalt not covet.

The above interpretation is a theological twisting of what the passage is actually saying. Those who hold to that interpretation make assumptions that cannot be supported by the text. In the context of Matt. 19, the rich ruler is not asking how to be saved from Hell so he can live in Heaven eternally. He is asking how to have quality of life, in the sense of reward and inheritance, in the coming kingdom. This man has apparently heard John the Baptist and Jesus preaching, *Repent, for the kingdom of heaven is at hand*. He desires to rule with Jesus in his heavenly kingdom. See the discussion in the previous chapter.

There are qualifications for inheriting the heavenly ruling realm of the kingdom. At the Judgment Seat all children of God will be rewarded according to works, and the reward will either be positive or negative. The young ruler has a distorted idea of what is required. So typical of the religious leadership of his day, he thinks that he must keep a list in order to qualify. In other words, if I do this and this and this, then I will inherit the kingdom and get that. So he wants to know from Jesus, "What is the list? What good thing must I do?"

His idea of being good is keeping a checklist. But this is legalism with respect to sanctification, which is just as wrong as legalism with respect to justification! It is a legal, contractual, entitlement approach to rewards, with the attitude, "Lord, if I keep my end of the bargain, then I am entitled to receive thus-and-such according to our legal agreement." It is the attitude of the first century Pharisees, and it is the attitude of this rich ruler, and an attitude prevalent in the church today. And it is just as wrong today as it was then. Spirituality is not obtained by checklist mentality. How does Jesus respond to this man's misunderstanding?

2. Christ's reply

Jesus begins by questioning the man's use of the word *good*. He calls Jesus, *Good Master*. The problem is, this man's idea of good is not God's idea of good. God is inherently good. But this man's idea of good is legalistic. He thinks that being good is based on outward behavior. For him, obedience is mechanical, and good is what comes of it. Perhaps in our times this would be a Christian who thinks that because he reads the Bible and goes to church and has conservative personal standards and doesn't kill anyone or commit adultery, he is therefore right with God and expects to be rewarded.

Do you see a problem with that mentality? Jesus certainly does, and it comes out in His reply. See the end of v. 17, *If thou wilt enter into life, keep the commandments*. In the Old Testament God promised life, quality of life, for those who would keep the law.

> Ye shall therefore keep my statutes, and my judgments: which if a man do, he shall live in them: I am the LORD. Lev. 18:5

Keeping the law never saved anyone from Hell, but obeying it brings vibrancy of spiritual life for those who are saved! That principle is corroborated in the New Testament as well.

> For to be carnally minded is death; but to be spiritually minded is life and peace. Because the carnal mind is enmity against God: for

> it is not subject to the law of God, neither indeed can be. So then
> they that are in the flesh cannot please God. Rom. 8:6-8

Obeying God brings vibrancy of spiritual life! Disobeying God results in death, not necessarily physical death, and certainly not eternal damnation, but spiritual stagnancy and withering.

If obeying the law of God brings vibrancy of life now and inheritance in the age of Messiah, then the ruler wants to know (v. 18) which aspects of the commandments Christ is referring to — moral? civil? ceremonial? Jesus narrows the field to the *moral* law. But we know He does not share the "keeping the list" mentality of the Jewish leadership of His day. In fact, in the Sermon on the Mount (Matt. 5-7), Jesus teaches the importance of obeying, not merely the letter of the law externally, but the spirit of the law internally. Consider the following example.

> Ye have heard that it was said by them of old time, Thou shalt not
> commit adultery: But I say unto you, That whosoever looketh on a
> woman to lust after her hath committed adultery with her already
> in his heart. Matt. 5:27-28

This is an expansion of understanding for the scribes and Pharisees. Thus, Jesus broadens the definition of obeying the law, from merely keeping a list outwardly, to obeying inwardly, from the heart — which is not characterized by a list but an attitude. Then Jesus teaches His disciples something astounding.

> Except your righteousness shall exceed the righteousness of the
> scribes and Pharisees, ye shall in no case enter into the kingdom of
> heaven. Matt. 5:20

How could anyone's righteousness exceed the righteousness of the scribes and Pharisees, seeing they kept the law so meticulously? The point is, they kept it outwardly, not inwardly; they were hypocrites. Not only that, but they added to the law their man-made traditions and then elevated those additions to the status of God's law. So if this rich ruler wants to enter the heavenly kingship, if he desires to rule and reign with Jesus, he must not merely keep the law outwardly, he must obey from the heart.

Not About Salvation From Condemnation

We must understand that if the man is merely asking about salvation and matters of endless life, then the answer Christ gives to him completely destroys salvation by faith alone. For Jesus tells the man that entrance (i.e., inheritance) in the kingdom is by obeying the law. Even if Jesus is emphasizing obedience from the heart, it is still works-based salvation. Of course, Jesus never advocated works-based salvation — not in this case or any other. This passage is not addressing matters of salvation from Hell in any respect. The focus is on matters of sanctification and discipleship unto eternal reward.

Those who superimpose their theological assumptions on this passage may view it as a salvation text, but that is contrary to the rules of hermeneutics. We must let the text speak for itself, not interpret through the lens of a theological system! Christ's encounter with the rich young ruler is not about salvation by grace through faith. The ruler wants to know how to be rewarded with a position in Christ's kingdom.

At this point in the dialogue, the ruler must be getting excited, for Jesus tells him that the way to enter into life is by keeping the commandments, namely the Ten Commandments (vs. 18-19). The young man is elated, for he claims he has kept the commandments since the time of his youth (v. 20). I personally think the man is expecting Jesus to say, "There is nothing else you must do. You qualify to inherit the kingdom!" Why would the ruler expect this? Because he is a legalist. He can honestly say he has kept the Ten Commandments as a sort of checklist. But then Jesus bursts the ruler's legalistic bubble. *If thou wilt be perfect, go and sell that thou hast, and give to the poor, and thou shalt have treasure in heaven: and come and follow me*, v. 21.

If thou wilt be perfect? The word means "fully mature." In a practical sense, it is the idea of going all the way in discipleship, of becoming an overcomer. Jesus is essentially saying to this rich young ruler, "If you want to be an overcomer, then go and sell your possessions and give the proceeds to the poor and needy. Then you will have treasure (special reward) in the heavenly realm of my kingdom." Again, Jesus is not promising the *gift* of eternal life. He is promising the *reward* of eternal life, entrance into the kingship, inheritance in the coming kingdom, residency in the city of reward.

What else must the man do? *Come and follow me.* The parallel passage in Mark 10:21 says, *Come, take up the cross, and follow me.* This is obviously not a call to salvation; it is a call to discipleship following salvation. Remarkably, Mark 10:21 says, *Jesus beholding him loved him,* and the word for love is *agapao* in Greek, the greatest kind of love, that is self-sacrificing and unconditional. Oh, the heart of Jesus! How He longs for us to follow Him.

Clearly, Jesus knows that the one thing the rich ruler values most in life is his wealth. Tragically, the man is unwilling to pay the high price of discipleship. The text says, *He went away sorrowful: for he had great possessions,* v. 22. He is unwilling to forsake all to follow Jesus. He is a moral man who keeps the law religiously, or we could say, legalistically. He keeps his checklist rigorously. But he is missing a deep communion and love for Christ and others. Wealth stands in the way. Is not his spiritual response summed up well in the parable of the four soils?

> The cares of this world, and the deceitfulness of riches, and the lusts of other things entering in, choke the word, and it becometh unfruitful. Mark 4:19

Oh, may we turn our eyes upon Jesus, look full in His wonderful face, so that the things of Earth will grow strangely dim in the light of His glory and grace.

After seeing the young man's sorrowful response, Jesus turns to His disciples and takes the opportunity to teach them.

> 23 Then said Jesus unto his disciples, Verily I say unto you, That a rich man shall hardly enter into the kingdom of heaven. 24 And again I say unto you, It is easier for a camel to go through the eye of a needle, than for a rich man to enter into the kingdom of God. Matt. 19:23-24

The word *hardly* means "with hardness," or "with great difficulty." In other words, it is very hard for a rich person to enter into the kingdom of the heavens, to qualify for ruling with Jesus. Why is that? It is not often that a rich person has an eternal worldview. Rather, they tend to depend on their wealth, their material resources, rather than Christ. When that is the case, they cannot enter (i.e., inherit) the kingdom. It's not impossible for wealthy people to enter the kingdom, but it is difficult or hard, like a camel going through the eye of a needle.

Through the Eye of the Needle

Some commentators insist this is referring to the eye of a sewing needle. But that does not fit the context, for Jesus is not saying it is *impossible* for the rich to enter; rather, it is *hard* for them to enter. What then is this illustration?

In ancient times cities were fortified to protect from enemies. A city would have massive gates for travelers to flow in and out of the city during the daytime, but at nighttime they would be closed. Only pedestrian traffic could go in and out through a much smaller gate, more like a doorway. It would be much safer for the city, for the soldiers could easily control the traffic flow.

When I was in Jerusalem, I saw these small doorways built into the city walls and our scholarly Jewish guide referred to them as the *eye of the needle*. In ancient times if a traveler arrived at night, after the large gates to the city had been closed, he could easily pass through the gate, but not his camel.

Suppose a traveler really wanted to get into the city at night, along with his camel. It could be done, but it was a very difficult process. First, the traveler would have to strip off all the baggage on the camel. He would then prod the camel to collapse down to a position of resting, with legs tucked underneath. But it's a great deal of work.

I have ridden on camels twice in my life — once in Israel and once in Jordan — and they are enormous creatures. One thing I really cannot imagine, but I've heard it can be done, is getting a camel that is collapsed down to scoot through a doorway, the eye of the needle. It's extremely difficult because, first, the doorway is so narrow and the camel is so wide. Not only that, but when the legs are tucked under the camel, it's really difficult for the camel to scoot. Nevertheless, with an enormous amount of coercing and prodding, the camel *can* make it through the eye of the needle.

It's that difficult for a rich man to enter into the kingdom of heaven. The reason is, the rich man has to strip off all his baggage, his dependence on wealth and resources. He has to get low, humbling himself, and with great difficulty keep his mind focused on the narrow doorway and getting through all during his life. There are so many distractions. Perhaps this is what Jesus meant when He said in Matt. 7:13-14, *Enter ye in at the strait gate: for ... strait is the gate, and narrow is the way, which leadeth unto life, and few there be that find it.*

Can a rich man inherit the kingdom? Yes! But with tremendous difficulty.

3. The disciples' questions

When the disciples hear how hard it is for a rich man to enter into the kingdom of the heavens, they have questions.

> When his disciples heard it, they were exceedingly amazed, saying, Who then can be saved? Matt. 19:25

When we see the word *saved,* our minds tend to think of salvation from eternal condemnation because we have a New Testament grid. But these Jews have an Old Testament grid. Of the numerous times the words *save, saved* and *salvation* are used in the Old Testament, hardly ever do they refer to eternal salvation from Hell. Almost always, these words take on the meaning of temporal deliverance of some sort. And the only time *eternal life* is used in the Old Testament is in relation to eternal rewards versus eternal shame (Dan. 12:2-3).

For these disciples to ask in a context dealing with earning eternal life, *Who then can be saved?* they are not thinking what we are thinking. Instead, they are wondering, "If inheritance in the kingdom is so difficult for those who are rich, then who can be delivered from their attachment to riches so they can enter the kingdom?" It is important to keep this within context. Jesus gives a glorious answer.

> With men this is impossible; but with God all things are possible. Matt. 19:26

A rich man cannot be delivered of his own strength. It is impossible without God, but with God it is possible. <u>The principle applies to anyone who is struggling with sin or has something standing in the way of full surrender</u>.

Peter then jumps into the discussion and asks what will be their portion as disciples, since they are not rich, and they have left all to follow Him.

> 27 Then answered Peter and said unto him, Behold, we have forsaken all, and followed thee; what shall we have therefore?
> 28 And Jesus said unto them, Verily I say unto you, That ye which have followed me, in the regeneration when the Son of man shall sit in the throne of his glory, ye also shall sit upon twelve thrones, judging the twelve tribes of Israel.
> 29 And every one that hath forsaken houses, or brethren, or sisters, or father, or mother, or wife, or children, or lands, for my name's sake, shall receive an hundredfold, and shall inherit everlasting life. Matt. 19:27-29

Jesus promises that in the regeneration His disciples will be rewarded with thrones, and they will rule over the twelve tribes of Israel. The *regeneration* is the Messianic restoration, the time when Messiah will rule on Earth and put things right again. What an honor! Incidentally, Jesus does not rebuke Peter for asking and confirms they will be rewarded abundantly for forsaking all and following Jesus.

There is also a promise for future disciples — i.e., those church age saints who are willing to pay the high price of discipleship. This applies to each of us. Whoever forsakes all to follow Jesus will *receive an hundredfold* and *inherit everlasting life*. Once again, this is not referring to salvation from eternal condemnation, or else it would be a works-based salvation. What this means is that those saints who make sacrifices for Jesus and forsake all to follow Him will be abundantly rewarded. The parallel Mark passage says both *now* and in the *age to come*! It is not a promise of material prosperity, but the Lord will prosper you spiritually now, if you follow Him, and He will reward you over-and-above at the Judgment Seat. Peter repeated this principle in his second epistle.

> Give diligence to make your calling and election sure ... For so an entrance shall be ministered unto you abundantly into the everlasting kingdom of our Lord and Saviour Jesus Christ. 2 Peter 1:10-11

We have come full circle and return to where we started. *Many that are first shall be last; and the last shall be first*, Matt. 19:30. Does this statement now make more sense? It means those who are first in this life — first in status and position, first in wealth and opportunity — will be last when it comes to kingdom inheritance. But those who are last in this life, because they give up those things for Christ's sake, will be first in the coming kingdom.

4. The parabolic conclusion

Now the parable of the entitled workers can be properly understood in its context, for ch. 20 is a continuation of ch. 19. Technically, there should be no chapter break.

> 1 For the kingdom of heaven is like unto a man that is an householder, which went out early in the morning to hire labourers into his vineyard.
> 2 And when he had agreed with the labourers for a penny a day, he sent them into his vineyard.
> 3 And he went out about the third hour, and saw others standing idle in the marketplace,
> 4 And said unto them; Go ye also into the vineyard, and whatsoever is right I will give you. And they went their way.
> 5 Again he went out about the sixth and ninth hour, and did likewise.
> 6 And about the eleventh hour he went out, and found others standing idle, and saith unto them, Why stand ye here all the day idle?
> 7 They say unto him, Because no man hath hired us. He saith unto them, Go ye also into the vineyard; and whatsoever is right, that shall ye receive.
> 8 So when even was come, the lord of the vineyard saith unto his steward, Call the labourers, and give them their hire, beginning from the last unto the first.
> 9 And when they came that were hired about the eleventh hour, they received every man a penny.
> 10 But when the first came, they supposed that they should have received more; and they likewise received every man a penny.
> 11 And when they had received it, they murmured against the goodman of the house,
> 12 Saying, These last have wrought but one hour, and thou hast made them equal unto us, which have borne the burden and heat of the day.
> 13 But he answered one of them, and said, Friend, I do thee no wrong: didst not thou agree with me for a penny?

14 Take that thine is, and go thy way: I will give unto this last, even as unto thee.
15 Is it not lawful for me to do what I will with mine own? Is thine eye evil, because I am good?
16 So the last shall be first, and the first last: for many be called, but few chosen. Matt. 20:1-16

The new chapter starts out, *For the kingdom of heaven is like.* Jesus is now going to describe some aspect of inheritance in the heavenly kingdom. Let me briefly tell the parable.

A common workday in the New Testament era was twelve hours, from 6:00 am to 6:00 pm. A vineyard owner goes into the marketplace to hire workers to harvest his grapes. He arrives early, before the workday begins, perhaps as early as 5:30 am. He locates his first group of workers and hires them for a negotiated amount of a penny a day, which is the average wage of their day. The workers agree with the vineyard owner, and they start work at 6:00 am.

At the third hour, or 9:00 am, the vineyard owner finds several more workers available in the marketplace and hires them. But notice in v. 4 that no specified amount of pay is negotiated. He simply says to them, *Whatsoever is right I will give you.* They also seem content and go to work.

The vineyard owner hires more workers at the sixth hour and the ninth hour, or 12:00 pm and 3:00 pm. Then finally, at the eleventh hour, or 5:00 pm, he hires still more workers for the last hour of the day. They have been standing available all day in the marketplace, waiting to be hired. He tells them in v. 7, *Whatsoever is right, that shall ye receive.* In fact, he communicates the same message about payment to every group except for the first. The first group is hired at a negotiated rate.

At 6:00 pm, it is quitting time, and all the men are paid. Curiously, the steward starts by paying the last workers first, that is, the ones hired last. Remarkably, these workers who had completely trusted the vineyard owner to do right by them, find that he blesses them abundantly, with a full day's wages for their one hour of work.

When the first group of workers step up to the cashier for their pay, they expect to receive more because they see the last group of workers hired have received a penny. They expect to receive at least twelve pennies each, a penny per hour of work. But they are shocked when the steward gives them only one penny. In fact, they are upset! Notice in vs. 10-12 they murmur about it and complain that they have worked twelve hours, enduring the heat of the day, only to receive the same rate of pay as those hired in the last hour.

Think about this parable for a minute. Jesus is illustrating some aspect of rewards as they relate to the kingdom of the heavens. If rewards are a legal payment of sorts for every hour of work done or every act of service performed, then we would expect the vineyard owner to agree with these workers and pay them their due. But that is not how God has set up the system of rewards. It is not a labor contract, paying you for your daily service on His behalf, which is your reasonable service. No! God's rewards are an act of His grace and love in which He bestows upon you what He sees fit, based on your loving labor for Him.

A "You Owe Me" Attitude

Here is the key, I believe, to understanding the parable. The focus is not on the amount of pay. The focus is on the attitude of the workers. The workers hired after the first round are all rewarded more graciously because of their attitude. They don't have the attitude that we must negotiate our pay with the boss. They don't have the attitude that we expect equal compensation with everyone else. They don't have the attitude that the boss has a legal requirement to us. That is indeed the attitude of the first group, but not of the other groups. The men hired at the third, sixth, ninth, and eleventh hours have all completely trusted the vineyard owner to treat them rightly, as He sees fit. The men hired at the beginning of the day, in contrast, have a legal attitude toward their pay — a "you owe me" attitude — the same attitude as the rich young ruler who has kept his list and expects compensation.

Those who have a "you owe me" attitude are legalists — in our era, Christian legalists who expect that God owes them. Because of their attitude, the first are made last. How are they first? In the parable, they are first in order of hiring, but more importantly — and this is the point of the parable — they are first in their "you owe me" attitude. They do not labor out of love and trust, like the others. They labor out of a legal, contractual arrangement that expects something in return. It is an entitlement mentality.

In like manner, large segments of evangelical Christianity believe that *all* Christians are overcomers and, therefore, *all* Christians will be rewarded at the Judgment Seat. Isn't that expectation very similar to the first group of workers hired in this parable? I wonder if they will have the same response at the Judgment Seat, when they are made to be last one day with respect to kingdom rewards. I wonder if they will be as upset and jealous of others who receive more. I wonder if they will question the goodness of God, as in v. 15. If so, it will be because their expectations are wrong, completely unbiblical.

The point of this parable is that we should forsake all to serve our great God and the Lord Jesus Christ, out of a heart of love, because He first loved us. It is certainly fine to desire rewards because God has offered them to us out of His heart of love. But like the workers hired at later hours in this parable, we should completely trust Him to do what is right and best at the Judgment Seat, knowing that He is a good and gracious Master. We should never worry about our reward, especially in comparison to the reward of others. And may we never have the legalistic attitude of much of Christianity that thinks that God has a legal obligation, more or less, to all those who are saved. What a terrible attitude! The last shall be first and the first last. *For many are called, but few are chosen.*

Chapter 7

Lost and Found

Parables of the Lost Coin, Lost Sheep, Lost Son, Two Sons
Luke 15; Matt. 21:28-32

Do you own a vehicle that is completely paid for? If so, have you ever lost your keys to that vehicle? Did you assume that, because you had lost your keys, you no longer owned the vehicle? Of course not! Losing the keys doesn't mean the vehicle ceases to be yours. It simply means you have lost the ability to use that vehicle to the fullest extent.

Have you ever lost a young child, perhaps at the store, or at the flea market, or in some other public place? Many years ago when our children were little, we went into an Amish farmer's market in Lancaster, PA. Our daughter Anna, who was probably only three or four years old at the time, ended up missing after letting go of Grandpa's hand and drifting away from him. Thankfully, we found her after several minutes of searching, tears streaming down her little face. The poor thing was so frightened. Yet, even while she was lost, she was still our child.

I would suggest that is how the word *lost* is used in the following text. Something owned was lost and later found, never ceasing to be the property of the owner while it was lost.

1 Then drew near unto him all the publicans and sinners for to hear him.
2 And the Pharisees and scribes murmured, saying, This man receiveth sinners, and eateth with them.
3 And he spake this parable unto them, saying,
4 What man of you, having an hundred sheep, if he lose one of them, doth not leave the ninety and nine in the wilderness, and go after that which is lost, until he find it?
5 And when he hath found it, he layeth it on his shoulders, rejoicing.
6 And when he cometh home, he calleth together his friends and neighbours, saying unto them, Rejoice with me; for I have found my sheep which was lost.
7 I say unto you, that likewise joy shall be in heaven over one sinner that repenteth, more than over ninety and nine just persons, which need no repentance.
8 Either what woman having ten pieces of silver, if she lose one piece, doth not light a candle, and sweep the house, and seek diligently till she find it?
9 And when she hath found it, she calleth her friends and her neighbours together, saying, Rejoice with me; for I have found the piece which I had lost.
10 Likewise, I say unto you, there is joy in the presence of the angels of God over one sinner that repenteth. Luke 15:1-10

A shepherd loses one of his sheep, and a woman loses one of her coins. The sheep belonged to the shepherd before it was lost, and it remained the shepherd's even while it was lost. The same applies to the woman and her coin.

It is critical to understand the correct meaning of the word *lost* in this text because it affects our interpretation of these parables and, in particular, the meaning of v. 10. I would submit that the "one sinner that repents" in v. 10 is not an unbeliever who gets saved. It is important to remember that the focus of the Synoptic Gospels is not evangelistic. Rather, Matthew, Mark and Luke are focused on national Israel — saved Israelites — repenting of their sins and getting right with Jehovah God from whom they have wandered in disobedience.

Therefore, we must be careful in our exposition of Luke 15 not to *gospelize* this text, that is, we must not make it a salvation text. It is a sanctification text, as we shall see. The key is in understanding the words *lost* and *sinner*.

Have you ever known any sinning saints — believers in Christ living for themselves rather than the Lord? Have you known saints who were wandering in sin away from the Lord and, in that sense, were lost?

The Meaning of *Lost*

The word *lost* (Gr., *apollumi*) according to Greek lexicons, has a range of meaning, depending on context. Following are some of the ways *apollumi* is translated in the New Testament.

1. To destroy or kill or be put to death. In Matt. 2:13 the angel of the Lord appeared to Joseph in a dream, saying, *Arise, and take the young child and his mother, and flee into Egypt, and be thou there until I bring thee word: for Herod will seek the young child to destroy him.*

2. To perish. John 3:16, *For God so loved the world, that he gave his only begotten Son, that whosoever believeth in him should not perish, but have everlasting life.*

3. To be deprived of something. Matt. 10:42, *Whosoever shall give to drink unto one of these little ones a cup of cold water only in the name of a disciple ... he shall in no wise lose his reward.*

4. To be lost — such as the lost sheep or the lost coin. For example, in Matt. 10:6 Jesus tells the disciples to go to the *lost* sheep of the house of Israel. Also Luke 19:10, *For the Son of man is come to seek and to save that which was lost.*

It is also important to get a correct understanding of the words *save* and *salvation* if we would rightly divide the parables and the Synoptic Gospels. We sometimes speak of an unsaved person as being lost. For example, 2 Cor. 4:3, *But if our gospel be hid, it is hid to them that are lost.* However, in the Synoptic Gospels the word is not used in this way.

The tendency for many is to assume the word *lost* always means eternally condemned. That is a hermeneutical mistake, for the word *lost* is rarely used in the Scriptures of unsaved people. The preponderance of times the word *lost* is used in the New Testament of a spiritual condition, is of saved people who are floundering in sin. They have wandered away from the Lord, and in that sense, they are lost. I would submit to you that any saved person who is living in carnality is lost to some degree and needs to be found, that is, they need to repent and return to the Lord.

Two Groups of Saved Sinners

Jesus repeatedly encounters two groups of sinners in Israel that are saved, but in need of repentance. They are polar opposites in one respect, but very much alike in another. The first group, comprised of scribes and Pharisees, are the self-righteous fundamentalists of Jesus' day. They are more focused on the letter of the law than the spirit of the law, fully expecting their keeping of lists and standards to make them spiritual. Priding themselves in strict observance of the law, they condescend to those who have "lesser standards." *God, I thank thee, that I am not as other men are, extortioners, unjust, adulterers, or even as this publican,* Matt. 18:11. Instead of comparing themselves to God and seeing how far they are from Him in fellowship, they compare themselves to "sinful" people and feel good about their spiritual condition. They are self-righteous and hypocritical. God wants us to compare ourselves to His Word, not to others, for we can always find some who are not as "good" as we are.

At the other end of the spectrum are the publicans (tax collectors) and harlots (immoral persons). The publicans and harlots represent the vice-like sinners within the nation, those who are living licentiously. For those who insist these seedier elements of society must be eternally lost, consider the present day church of Jesus Christ, which is plagued by many who are saved, yet living in fornication or adultery or drunkenness, or other sins. Indeed, in 1 Cor. 6:15 Paul warns the Corinthian believers that their bodies are the members of Christ and not to be the members of harlots.

Jesus treats both groups — scribes and Pharisees, on the one end; publicans and harlots, on the other — as "sinners." But He never calls into question their eternal standing with God. He does, however, deem them both *lost* and in need of repentance.

Doesn't the use of the word *lost* imply they are eternally condemned and in need of eternal life? That is an assumption made by many, but it is not consistent with the Synoptic Gospels. Jesus refers to both groups as if eternally saved, but in need of restored fellowship with God. That can be clearly demonstrated from another parable.

Parable of the Two Sons

28 But what think ye? A certain man had two sons; and he came to the first, and said, Son, go work to day in my vineyard.

29 He answered and said, I will not: but afterward he repented, and went.

30 And he came to the second, and said likewise. And he answered and said, I go, sir: and went not.

31 Whether of them twain did the will of his father? They say unto him, The first. Jesus saith unto them, Verily I say unto you, That the publicans and the harlots go into the kingdom of God before you.

32 For John came unto you in the way of righteousness, and ye believed him not: but the publicans and the harlots believed him: and ye, when ye had seen it, repented not afterward, that ye might believe him. Matt. 21:28-32

Notice in the parable the vineyard owner has two *sons*. Sonship is evidence of an eternally secure relationship with God. Furthermore, both sons are asked to work in the Father's vineyard, again, evidence of right positional standing with God. The first son initially refuses to work in his father's vineyard, but he later repents and goes. According to the interpretation given by Jesus, this son represents the publicans and harlots who are not right with God at first but later repent when they hear John's message of repentance. The other son agrees to work for his father, but then never does. This latter son epitomizes the hypocritical religious leaders, namely the scribes and Pharisees, who claim to be doing the will of God, but whose self-righteous hearts are not right with Him.

Imagine how infuriated the Pharisees become when Jesus announces the publican and harlots will go into the kingdom of God before them. Why will this happen? Because the publicans and harlots have believed the message of John and repented of their lifestyle. Of course, the Pharisees are sinners too, but they can't see their spiritual need and so do not repent.

Interestingly, Jesus assumes that both groups — the scribes and Pharisees and the publicans and harlots — will be *in* the kingdom, but the repentant publicans and harlots will *go before* (precede) the unrepentant Pharisees, signifying a greater status in the kingdom for those who are repentant. As a result of bringing forth the fruits of repentance, the righteousness of the publicans and harlots exceeds the righteousness of the scribes and Pharisees. The publicans and harlots, now revived, will be *great* in the millennial kingdom, while the scribes and Pharisees will be *least* (Matt. 5:19-20).

Back in our primary text in Luke 15, we find the same two polar groups of sinners — those guilty of vice-type sins (publican and sinners) and those guilty of self-righteousness (Pharisees and scribes). In both cases, they are *saved* sinners.

> 1 Then drew near unto him all the publicans and sinners for to hear him.
> 2 And the Pharisees and scribes murmured, saying, This man receiveth sinners, and eateth with them. Luke 15:1-2

Jesus is accused by the Pharisees, the self-righteous sinners, of eating with the vice sinners. So He tells them the parable of the lost sheep (see verses near beginning of this chapter). The shepherd owns one hundred sheep. They *all* belong to the shepherd. This pictures their standing before God as eternally secure. One of the sheep becomes lost by wandering. This does not mean he is suddenly unsaved, for it is impossible to lose salvation. In the metaphor, the sheep is an Israelite who wanders away from God through sinning. The Good Shepherd, Jesus Christ, goes after His lost sheep because He came to seek and to save that which was *lost*. Fight the urge. *Lost* here does not mean eternally condemned, as is so commonly taught. *Lost* here means eternally saved, but not right with God. That fact will be demonstrated further as we go along.

Just Persons That Need No Repentance

Jesus did not come to call righteous Israelites to repentance, those who were already in right fellowship with God. In v. 7, they are called *just persons, which need no repentance*. Some like to say the word *just* refers to positional righteousness, that is, justification. It does in some contexts, but not in this context. Here it refers to practical righteousness — that is, progressive sanctification — and that is consistent with other usages in the New Testament.

For instance, in Matt. 1:19 we learn of Joseph who, when he learns of Mary's pregnancy, is determined to put her away privately (i.e., not divorce her publicly) because he is a *just* man. That obviously doesn't mean he is saved, justified. It means he is a good, righteous man who acts uprightly in his everyday living. When Pilate washes his hands to demonstrate his innocence in the matter of judging Jesus, he says, *I am innocent of the blood of this just person*, Matt. 27:24. Pilate is obviously not saying Jesus is eternally justified in the eyes of God. He is saying that Jesus is innocent, upright. So context must determine how the word *just* is being used.

Thus in context, v. 7 is saying Heaven rejoices whenever Christians get right with God. There's undoubtedly also joy in Heaven when eternally lost people become eternally saved, but that's not the point here.

The imagery of the woman and the ten coins is similar to the shepherd and his sheep. The woman owns all ten coins, just as the shepherd owns all the sheep. The fact that one sheep or one coin is lost, does not mean the shepherd or the woman no longer own what is rightfully theirs. It simply means one is temporarily lost and needs to be found. In both cases, though, notice the aggressiveness with which the owners go after what is theirs. Obviously, out of a heart of love, Jesus goes after His sheep that are wandering, whether they are first century Israelites or twenty-first century Christians.

As an aside, why do you suppose angels are joyful about Christians getting right with God? Think about it. One day, Satan and his host of angels will be deposed by Christ, and Jesus will rule in His kingdom, along with those saints who have lived uprightly. God's holy angels are eager to see Satan deposed and righteousness ruling on Earth. Unrepentant saints are counterproductive to that goal because they are not becoming qualified to rule and reign together with Jesus. The same Earth that is today ruled by Satan and his host will one day be ruled by faithful saints, with Christ as the ultimate ruler. When we are not living for God, we are not preparing ourselves for our ultimate purpose of glorifying God by ruling over Earth. So angels are joyful when saints get right with God and stay right with God.

The Prodigal

Jesus shares a third parable in Luke 15 that illustrates the same truth that repentance of first century national Israelites has nothing to do with salvation from eternal condemnation.

11 And he said, A certain man had two sons:
12 And the younger of them said to his father, Father, give me the portion of goods that falleth to me. And he divided unto them his living.
13 And not many days after the younger son gathered all together, and took his journey into a far country, and there wasted his substance with riotous living.
14 And when he had spent all, there arose a mighty famine in that land; and he began to be in want.
15 And he went and joined himself to a citizen of that country; and he sent him into his fields to feed swine.
16 And he would fain have filled his belly with the husks that the swine did eat: and no man gave unto him.
17 And when he came to himself, he said, How many hired servants of my father's have bread enough and to spare, and I perish with hunger!
18 I will arise and go to my father, and will say unto him, Father, I have sinned against heaven, and before thee,
19 And am no more worthy to be called thy son: make me as one of thy hired servants. Luke 15:11-19

The prodigal, despite his profligate living, is the father's son throughout the entire parable. Most commentators understand the father in this parable to represent our heavenly Father. If saved, you are His son, and nothing can take away that relationship from you. Regardless of your lifestyle, you will always be a child of God. Behavior does not determine your eternal standing with God. If it did, then you would continually doubt your salvation. Frankly, that is why many Calvinists and Arminians constantly doubt their salvation, because they make salvation contingent on behavior. That is theologically erroneous and destroys the gospel of faith alone.

This son is a *son*! Nothing can change that. He is a saved Israelite and, therefore, enjoys an unconditional inheritance as a child of God, namely, eternal life. The same is true of you, dear Christian. However, there is also a conditional inheritance, one that is not guaranteed, the status of firstborn sons, which allows us the privilege of ruling and reigning with

Christ. But there are qualifications. Rom. 8:17 says, *And if children, then heirs; heirs of God, and joint-heirs with Christ; if so be that we suffer with him, that we may be also glorified together.* Notice very carefully in the verse that ruling with Christ as a joint-heir and being glorified together with Him are conditional. The conditional inheritance can be squandered away by riotous living and an unwillingness to pay the price of discipleship. But thankfully, God always has open arms to receive back wayward saints. And all Heaven rejoices over their return.

Of course, the son is not the focus of the prodigal son story. The focus is on the Father.

20 And he arose, and came to his father. But when he was yet a great way off, his father saw him, and had compassion, and ran, and fell on his neck, and kissed him.
21 And the son said unto him, Father, I have sinned against heaven, and in thy sight, and am no more worthy to be called thy son.
22 But the father said to his servants, Bring forth the best robe, and put it on him; and put a ring on his hand, and shoes on his feet:
23 And bring hither the fatted calf, and kill it; and let us eat, and be merry:
24 For this my son was dead, and is alive again; he was lost, and is found. And they began to be merry. Luke 15:20-24

Don't miss the imagery. The prodigal son is a son! He represents a saved man, secure in his eternal relationship with God. But by sinning he sullies his fellowship with God. When he repents, the Father eagerly receives him back. However, our Father in heaven is not eager to receive back to fellowship unrepentant saints. His reception is based on repentance.

Notice the heart attitude of the repentant son in v. 18-19, *Father, I have sinned against heaven, and before thee, and am no more worthy to be called thy son: make me as one of thy hired servants.* The son's repentance prompts the father to use the same terminology we have seen elsewhere — *This my son was dead, and is alive again; he was lost, and is found,* v. 24. This is a saved sinner — a son! — getting right with God. The fact that he became lost cannot mean he became unsaved or was never saved in the first place. In context, it *must* mean that as a son he wandered away, out of fellowship, but the moment he repented he was restored to fellowship with his father. Glory!

Aren't you grateful that your loving heavenly Father is always ready and willing to receive you back home? Aren't you thankful that He is eager to kill the fatted calf and celebrate your return? Isn't it wonderful that all Heaven rejoices over sinning saints returning back home? Of course, it is all predicated on repentance.

The Other Son

There is one other aspect to the story we must consider: the other son. He stays home and does not waste his life in riotous living. However, he has an attitude.

> 25 Now his elder son was in the field: and as he came and drew nigh to the house, he heard musick and dancing.
> 26 And he called one of the servants, and asked what these things meant.
> 27 And he said unto him, Thy brother is come; and thy father hath killed the fatted calf, because he hath received him safe and sound.
> 28 And he was angry, and would not go in: therefore came his father out, and intreated him.
> 29 And he answering said to his father, Lo, these many years do I serve thee, neither transgressed I at any time thy commandment: and yet thou never gavest me a kid, that I might make merry with my friends:
> 30 But as soon as this thy son was come, which hath devoured thy living with harlots, thou hast killed for him the fatted calf.
> 31 And he said unto him, Son, thou art ever with me, and all that I have is thine.
> 32 It was meet that we should make merry, and be glad: for this thy brother was dead, and is alive again; and was lost, and is found. Luke 15:25-32

The prodigal son represents the publicans and harlots who get right with God. This other son represents the scribes and Pharisees whose outward life is conforming, but inwardly, there is a bad attitude that betrays their spiritual corruption. I believe this is the attitude of many legalistic Christians, perhaps the fundamentalists of our day. "Lord, we have been faithful," they would proclaim, but God knows it is grit-your-teeth-try-harder-flesh-dependent faithfulness. "Lord, we have been obedient," but the Lord sees it as outward conformity, not genuine, inward obedience. Like this other son, many have the attitude: "You never threw a party for us! But as soon as "bad boy" comes home after sowing his wild oats, you roll out the red carpet and treat him as if he were the first-born."

Back in v. 12 we learn the prodigal is the *younger* son, so he should not have the birthright, the status of firstborn son. Nevertheless, at the reception in v. 22, the father puts on him the best robe and a ring on his hand. This is the Father's signet ring, a very important emblem of firstborn inheritance. In other words, the father confers upon the prodigal son, now repentant, the status of firstborn son. Though he is younger, he gets the birthright because of his repentance and sweet, humble spirit. He gets the conditional inheritance, the reward, a double portion of the father's assets. After the father's death, he will administer the affairs of the household, in the father's stead. He will also be the spiritual ruler of the family.

Is the father rewarding this son's licentious living? By no means! He is rewarding his repentance and change of life and complete dedication to the father. The prodigal — now transformed! — sees himself as unworthy (v. 19), but the Father essentially says, "Because of your attitude and repentant heart, I consider you worthy of the status of a firstborn son." The self-righteous son who had stayed home, though he had been born first, is stripped of the status of firstborn son. It is now given to the younger. The Father assures the self-righteous son of his eternal security (the father's resources) in v. 31, but that is all. He does not have the ruling robe and he does not have the father's signet ring. He has forfeited the inheritance of a firstborn son. And so will you, child of God, if you do not repent and live the rest of your days in righteousness, not merely self-righteousness.

Throughout this text in Luke 15, the Greek word (*huios*) for a mature son is used of both sons. Yet in the very end, when the father disinherits the self-righteous son in v. 31, he says to him, *Son, thou art ever with me, and all that I have is thine.* Remarkably, the father switches the Greek word for *son* to *teknon,* which is the word used of immature, non-inheriting sons. This is yet another evidence that the self-righteous son has been demoted in status and disinherited as firstborn. What a dreadful loss!

What's the point of this parable? As a child of God, you are eternally secure. Nothing can take that away from you. But if you do not repent of your sinful ways and walk in faithfulness before the Lord, you will never be rewarded with the status of a firstborn son. You will be disinherited and not be able to fulfill the purpose for which you were created, which is to glorify God by ruling with Christ in His coming kingdom. As children of God, we should all take heed. The apostle John summed it up well, *Look to yourselves, that we lose not those things which we have wrought, but that we receive a full reward,* 2 John 8.

Zacchaeus: A Classic Illustration of Lost and Found

In closing, let's see an actual person in the New Testament who was lost and becomes found.

> And Jesus entered and passed through Jericho. And, behold, there was a man named Zacchaeus, which was the chief among the publicans, and he was rich. Luke 19:1-2

Publicans were Jews who collected taxes for the Roman government, which would look aside if the publicans padded the amount due and kept the excess for themselves. All the Romans cared about was the tax due to the government.

Zacchaeus is a wealthy man because he is a thief. He is not a self-righteous sinner like the Pharisees. He is a vice-sinner, a man of questionable moral behavior. That is why in v. 7 the people murmur, saying that Jesus is going to be the guest of a sinner — not an unsaved man, but a sinning saint of Israel.

What happens to Zacchaeus the day he meets Jesus? The traditional answer is to gospelize and say that he gets saved from eternal condemnation. But those who take this position *assume* that salvation precedes Zacchaeus' repentance, despite the fact the text says nothing about his salvation. It seems more likely that Zacchaeus is a regenerate man who repents, not an unsaved man who gets saved. Notice what happens.

> And Zacchaeus stood, and said unto the Lord; Behold, Lord, the half of my goods I give to the poor; and if I have taken any thing from any man by false accusation, I restore him fourfold. Luke 19:8

Is that the way to get saved from eternal condemnation? If so, then salvation is by works, yet we know from the overwhelming testimony of Scripture, salvation is by faith alone. Notice what Jesus says to Zacchaeus:

> And Jesus said unto him, This day is salvation come to this house, forsomuch as he also is a son of Abraham. For the Son of man is come to seek and to save that which was lost. Luke 19:9-10

Resist the urge to conclude that salvation must always be from eternal condemnation. And resist the urge to conclude that a lost person in the gospels is always unsaved (in an eternal sense). We must shatter our preconceived notions and admit that a first century Jew — who would have had an Old Testament psyche, not a New Testament grid — would not have thought of salvation in the sense of obtaining eternal life. That was *not* typically how the word *saved* or *salvation* was used in the Old Testament. The words *save* and *salvation* are virtually always used in the Old Testament to suggest deliverance of some sort — deliverance from enemies; deliverance from problems; deliverance from God's temporal judgment; even deliverance from self — but not deliverance from eternal condemnation.

We must conclude that Zacchaeus is a saved Israelite who repents of his sinfulness and gets right with God when He meets Jesus. He has undoubtedly already heard the message of John the Baptist, urging Jews to repent in the spirit of 2 Chron. 7:14. He knows he is a thief and apparently becomes overwhelmed with conviction in the presence of Jesus. And so he humbles himself and is restored to fellowship with Jehovah God.

Adding further credence to what I am proposing is the parable Jesus tells the audience at that very point, starting in Luke 19:11. It is the parable of the pounds, a parable about rewards for faithful Christians! That parable would be out of place and confusing if Zacchaeus had gotten saved from eternal condemnation. For salvation is by faith alone. But reward is according to works.

Zacchaeus is transformed! He is revived! And his heart response is the typical response of a revived saint. He wants to make right all the wrongs in his life so he can be clean before God and be rewarded at the Judgment Seat.

If today, as a child of God, you are *lost*, wandering away from the Lord, living in sinfulness — whether vice-like sin or pious, hypocritical sin — then repent and submit to the Holy Spirit, who is out looking for you. The Hound of Heaven is on your trail!

Chapter 8

Chop Down the Tree

Parable of the Unfruitful Fig
Luke 13:1-9

On Main Street, heading out of our town, is a privately-owned billboard. It pictures people walking down the road of life, heading toward flames in the distance, obviously representing Hell. The caption quotes the words of Jesus, "Unless you repent you will all perish" (Luke 13:3). While I appreciate the evangelistic heartbeat of the owner of the billboard, he actually misuses the verse and sends the wrong message about the Gospel. For that matter, a large segment of evangelical Christianity misinterprets this section of Luke 13, using it as a salvation from Hell text. But is Jesus speaking about eternal condemnation? Let's examine this text and see.

> 1 There were present at that season some that told him of the Galilaeans, whose blood Pilate had mingled with their sacrifices.
> 2 And Jesus answering said unto them, Suppose ye that these Galilaeans were sinners above all the Galilaeans, because they suffered such things?
> 3 I tell you, Nay: but, except ye repent, ye shall all likewise perish.
> 4 Or those eighteen, upon whom the tower in Siloam fell, and slew them, think ye that they were sinners above all men that dwelt in Jerusalem?
> 5 I tell you, Nay: but, except ye repent, ye shall all likewise perish.

6 He spake also this parable; A certain man had a fig tree planted in his vineyard; and he came and sought fruit thereon, and found none.

7 Then said he unto the dresser of his vineyard, Behold, these three years I come seeking fruit on this fig tree, and find none: cut it down; why cumbereth it the ground?

8 And he answering said unto him, Lord, let it alone this year also, till I shall dig about it, and dung it:

9 And if it bear fruit, well: and if not, then after that thou shalt cut it down. Luke 13:1-9

Jesus begins with a current event in v. 1. Some Jewish Galileans had traveled to the temple in Jerusalem to offer sacrifices. They may have been revolutionaries that Rome was trying to arrest. We don't really know. But what we do know is that Pilate kills them at the temple, and their blood becomes mingled with the blood of the sacrifices. Whether Pilate was justified in killing them or not, we cannot conclude, but Jesus uses the event to ask His audience a question in v. 2. To paraphrase, "Do you suppose these Galileans died prematurely because they were more sinful than their countrymen?" The answer is no, we cannot make that determination. Only God knows.

Jesus uses another current event in v. 4. Siloam is an area of Jerusalem where the Pool of Siloam is located. Some accident had occurred, involving a tower that had fallen, causing the deaths of eighteen people. This would have been big news in Jerusalem. Jesus inquires, "Do you suppose these citizens of Jerusalem were more sinful than others who lived in Jerusalem, and that is why they died prematurely?" Again, the answer is no, we have no way of knowing. Only God knows the condition of their heart. They could have been upright people, for all we know.

What is the point being made by Jesus? "Unless you repent, you will all perish." The assumption typically made by those who are preaching or teaching this passage is that *to perish* means to go to Hell. But is that justified? It is not, for the Greek word merely means, "to suffer destruction." In this context, it means to die. In fact, it is the same Greek word used by the disciples when they were in the boat with Jesus on the Sea of Galilee and a magnificent storm arose, tossing them about. Fearing for their lives, they awakened Jesus and asked, *Master, carest thou not that we perish?* Mark 4:38. Were the disciples assuming they would go to Hell? No, and neither are these Jews in Christ's audience.

The word *perish*, in this context, simply means to die; it is physical death and has nothing to do with going to Hell. Isn't that what happened to these Galileans killed by Pilate and these bystanders killed by the falling tower? They died. Dare we suggest they went to Hell? What characterizes both groups is that they died prematurely. And so Jesus is making the point to His Jewish listeners that they, too, will die prematurely if they do not repent.

Why does Jesus emphasize repentance so strongly? As we have seen throughout this book, it is because His focus in the Synoptic Gospels is to call national Israel back to fellowship with Jehovah God, from whom they have wandered. God had promised to receive back His erring nation if they would turn from their sins and return to the Lord.

> Take heed unto yourselves, lest ye forget the covenant of the LORD your God, which he made with you ... For the LORD thy God is a consuming fire, even a jealous God. When thou shalt beget children, and children's children, and ye shall have remained long in the land, and shall corrupt yourselves ... and shall do evil in the sight of the LORD thy God, to provoke him to anger: I call heaven and earth to witness against you this day, that ye shall soon utterly perish from off the land whereunto ye go over Jordan to possess it; ye shall not prolong your days upon it, but shall utterly be destroyed. And the LORD shall scatter you among the nations, and ye shall be left few in number among the heathen, whither the LORD shall lead you ... But if from thence thou shalt seek the LORD thy God, thou shalt find him, if thou seek him with all thy heart and with all thy soul. When thou art in tribulation, and all these things are come upon thee, even in the latter days, if thou turn to the LORD thy God, and shalt be obedient unto his voice; (For the LORD thy God is a merciful God;) he will not forsake thee, neither destroy thee, nor forget the covenant of thy fathers which he sware unto them. Deut. 4:23-31

Another parallel text to the above is 2 Chron. 7:13-14, which we mentioned earlier. Of course, these promises have nothing to do with Israel becoming saved from eternal Hell. They are about returning to fellowship with the Father, lest judgment come upon the nation. In the New Testament context of Luke 13, the judgment would come in the form of premature death. As we know from history, Israel refused to repent, and Jerusalem was destroyed by Rome less than four decades after the time of Christ. How do we know Jesus is prophetically referring to the destruction of Jerusalem? The parable leads to this conclusion.

A man plants a fig tree in his vineyard, and even after three years when it should be bearing fruit, it is not. Why three years? Perhaps this is a reference to Christ's three-year ministry urging the nation to repent. In the parable, after allowing three years and still finding no fruit, the owner of the vineyard orders the fig to be cut down, making way for other fruit-bearing trees to be planted. The gardener intervenes and asks the owner to give it another year — or we could say, an extended period of time — while he fertilizes and nurtures the tree, in an attempt to bring it to fruit-bearing. If after the extended period of time the tree is still not fruit-bearing, then it will be cut down.

The tree is national Israel. The gardener, seeking more time for the tree, is Jesus. God the Father is the owner of the vineyard. Cutting down the tree represents judgment upon the nation, the setting aside of Israel. We already saw the metaphor of a tree being cut down used by John the Baptist in Matt. 3:7-10. Casting of the tree into the fire seems prophetic of the Roman destruction. But why the waiting period of nearly forty years until national judgment? Why has the gardener asked for an extension of time?

> It is of the LORD'S mercies that we are not consumed, because his compassions fail not. Lam. 3:22

> Despisest thou the riches of his goodness and forbearance and longsuffering; not knowing that the goodness of God leadeth thee to repentance? Rom. 2:4

God is abundantly merciful, patient, and long-suffering. He gives all of His children opportunities to turn from their sinful ways before sending judgment. This parable is about God extending Israel's impending judgment, to permit the nation additional time to be restored to fellowship. Remarkably, God allows the *gospel of the kingdom* to be preached even *after* the death, burial, and resurrection of Jesus — but only for a limited time. In other words, even after Christ's ascension

back to heaven, the Jewish people are given additional opportunities to repent and receive an inheritance in the heavenly
kingdom. Where do we find this offer?

On the day of Pentecost, Peter stood before a mass
audience of Jews who had gathered in Jerusalem for the purpose of celebrating the feasts. His message is not for Gentiles
wanting to know how to be saved from Hell. That would
come later. What he says is directed at Jews who have, to this
point, rejected the call to, "Repent, for the kingdom of the
heavens is at hand." Notice Peter's unique message and the
profound response.

> 37 Now when they heard this, they were pricked in their heart,
> and said unto Peter and to the rest of the apostles, Men and
> brethren, what shall we do?
> 38 Then Peter said unto them, **Repent, and be baptized every one
> of you in the name of Jesus Christ for the remission of sins**, and
> ye shall receive the gift of the Holy Ghost.
> 39 For the promise is unto you, and to your children, and to all
> that are afar off, even as many as the Lord our God shall call.
> 40 And with many other words did he testify and exhort, saying,
> Save yourselves from this untoward generation.
> 41 Then they that gladly received his word were baptized: and the
> same day there were added unto them about three thousand souls.
> Acts 2:37-41 (emphasis added)

Evangelical preachers, teachers and commentators typically explain this event as three thousand Jews getting saved
from eternal condemnation. But that is not what is happening
here. How do we know? First, this message preached by Peter
is identical to the message preached by Jesus and John the
Baptist.

> John did baptize in the wilderness, and preach **the baptism of
> repentance for the remission of sins**. Mark 1:4

> And he came into all the country about Jordan, preaching **the
> baptism of repentance for the remission of sins**. Luke 3:3

> Then Peter said unto them, **Repent, and be baptized** every one of
> you in the name of Jesus Christ **for the remission of sins**, and ye
> shall receive the gift of the Holy Ghost. Acts 2:38 (emphasis added)

Second, Peter is speaking to a Jewish audience, and they
are devout (regenerated) men, who have come from the many

nations where they had previously been scattered as a result of the Assyrian invasion of 722 BC. *And there were dwelling at Jerusalem Jews, devout men, out of every nation under heaven*, Acts 2:5. They have come to Jerusalem to observe the Passover — fifty days prior to Pentecost — during which time Christ had been crucified. Many of them had undoubtedly seen the crucifixion, or at least heard about it. They have remained or returned for the feast of Pentecost.

Peter's message is not about how they can be saved from Hell. If it had been, he would have preached, as did Paul, "Believe on the Lord Jesus Christ and thou shalt be saved." But that is not what he preaches. Instead, he preaches, *Repent, and be baptized ... for the remission of sins, and ye shall receive the gift of the Holy Ghost*. Peter is essentially preaching in the spirit of Jer. 31 and letting these Jews know the New Covenant has arrived. But he also brings a stinging indictment upon his brethren.

> Ye men of Israel, hear these words; Jesus of Nazareth, a man approved of God among you by miracles and wonders and signs, which God did by him in the midst of you, as ye yourselves also know: Him, being delivered by the determinate counsel and foreknowledge of God, ye have taken, and by wicked hands have crucified and slain: Whom God hath raised up, having loosed the pains of death: because it was not possible that he should be holden of it. Acts 2:22-24

"You crucified Messiah, the Son of God!" Peter exclaims to a stunned audience. He then turns to Old Testament prophecy and reminds his countrymen of the Messianic promises made to King David. Indeed, Messiah had been prophesied to come from the seed of David.

> Men and brethren, let me freely speak unto you of the patriarch David, that he is both dead and buried, and his sepulchre is with us unto this day. Therefore being a prophet, and knowing that God had sworn with an oath to him, that of the fruit of his loins, according to the flesh, he would raise up Christ to sit on his throne; He seeing this before spake of the resurrection of Christ, that his soul was not left in hell, neither his flesh did see corruption. This Jesus hath God raised up, whereof we all are witnesses. Therefore being by the right hand of God exalted, and having received of the Father the promise of the Holy Ghost, he hath shed forth this, which ye now see and hear. Acts 2:29-33

This is a Jewish message, through and through. "God sent Jesus as the Messiah. He was the One sent to sit on the throne of David. He came to offer you inheritance in the kingdom of the heavens. But you crucified Him!" The Jewish audience is stricken with grief. *Now when they heard this, they were pricked in their heart, and said unto Peter and to the rest of the apostles, Men and brethren, what shall we do?* Acts 2:37. They come to realize they have killed the Messiah, and they are horrified. "What can we do about it?" they cry out. Peter says, "Repent and be baptized." In other words, "Turn from your sins, embrace Jesus as your Messiah, and become immersed in water to signify your cleansing and change of life."

This is not the gospel of grace, the good news as to how an eternally lost person is saved from condemnation. Incidentally, because so many insist that it is, errors in interpretation have resulted. For instance, many churches believe baptism is a requirement for salvation from Hell. That is horrific error, for eternal salvation is by faith alone. Most Protestants (including Baptists) insist baptism is *not* a requirement for eternal salvation. Nevertheless, they resort to interpretive gymnastics, tying to make the meaning of Peter's statements fit the gospel of grace message by faith alone. It's like putting a square peg in a round hole, which doesn't work. Misinterpretations of this nature disappear when interpreters realize Peter is not preaching the gospel of grace by faith alone. He is preaching the gospel of the kingdom, the good news that those saints who repent of their sins and live in fellowship with God will qualify to inherit the heavenly realm of the kingdom.

Let's now fast-forward a few years to Acts 3. Peter has just healed a man at the temple, and the people wonder at the sight of it. Peter wastes no time and starts preaching.

> And when Peter saw it, he answered unto the people, Ye men of Israel, why marvel ye at this? or why look ye so earnestly on us, as though by our own power or holiness we had made this man to walk? The God of Abraham, and of Isaac, and of Jacob, the God of our fathers, hath glorified his Son Jesus; whom ye delivered up, and denied him in the presence of Pilate, when he was determined to let him go. But ye denied the Holy One and the Just, and desired a murderer to be granted unto you; And killed the Prince of life, whom God hath raised from the dead; whereof we are witnesses.

And his name through faith in his name hath made this man strong, whom ye see and know: yea, the faith which is by him hath given him this perfect soundness in the presence of you all. And now, brethren, I wot that through ignorance ye did it, as did also your rulers. But those things, which God before had shewed by the mouth of all his prophets, that Christ should suffer, he hath so fulfilled. Acts 3:12-18

Again, Peter proclaims, "God sent Jesus as the Messiah, but you killed him! I know you did it in ignorance. You were zealous for God and thought Jesus was a fraud. But He was of God." After preaching about Jesus as Messiah, Peter calls his Jewish brethren to repentance.

Repent ye therefore, and be converted, that your sins may be blotted out, when the times of refreshing shall come from the presence of the Lord; And he shall send Jesus Christ, which before was preached unto you: Whom the heaven must receive until the times of restitution of all things, which God hath spoken by the mouth of all his holy prophets since the world began. Acts 3:19-21

The phrase, *times of refreshing*, is a direct reference to the Messianic kingdom. Later in the passage it is referred to again as, *the times of restitution of all things*. Peter is not preaching to unsaved people about how to get saved from eternal condemnation. He is preaching to covenant Jews, who are saved, about their need to turn back to Jehovah. They must, *Repent ... and be converted*. The word *converted* does not mean to become regenerated, as the word is often misused. It means "to revert, to turn again to a previous state." These Jews need to turn again to fellowship with the Lord, for they have wandered away from Him in disobedience. If they do not repent, then judgment will come upon the nation, as Peter warns in v. 23, *And it shall come to pass, that every soul, which will not hear that prophet, shall be destroyed from among the people.*

Now we fast-forward one more time to Acts 28. The year is AD 63 or 64. Paul is in Rome, in prison. In v. 20 he gives his primary purpose for being there: *For the hope of Israel I am bound with this chain*. What is the hope of Israel? In a general sense it is Jesus, but more specifically, it is the Messianic hope, the Messianic kingdom. Thus, God allows Paul to go to a Roman prison so he can preach the *gospel of the kingdom* to the Jews in Rome. In v. 17 we are told, *Paul called the chief of the*

Jews together. The sermon is a heartfelt appeal to his Jewish leadership.

> 23 And when they had appointed him a day, there came many to him into his lodging; to whom he expounded and testified the kingdom of God, persuading them concerning Jesus, both out of the law of Moses, and out of the prophets, from morning till evening.
> 24 And some believed the things which were spoken, and some believed not.
> 25 And when they agreed not among themselves, they departed, after that Paul had spoken one word, Well spake the Holy Ghost by Esaias the prophet unto our fathers,
> 26 Saying, Go unto this people, and say, Hearing ye shall hear, and shall not understand; and seeing ye shall see, and not perceive:
> 27 For the heart of this people is waxed gross, and their ears are dull of hearing, and their eyes have they closed; lest they should see with their eyes, and hear with their ears, and understand with their heart, and should be converted, and I should heal them.
> 28 Be it known therefore unto you, that the salvation of God is sent unto the Gentiles, and that they will hear it. Acts 28:23-28

The apostle teaches (v. 23) these Jewish leaders the *gospel of the kingdom*, attempting to convince them from the Scriptures that Jesus is indeed the Messianic hope. His message to them is the same as what Jesus and John the Baptist and Peter had preached to the Jews previously, for Paul quotes Isa. 6:9-10 in vs. 24-27. Jesus quoted those very words when announcing His reason for resorting to parables in Matt. 13:13-15.

What is Paul offering? Is it salvation from condemnation? No, the end of v. 27 indicates it is a message of conversion and healing. These Jews have been sickened by sin, which has disrupted their fellowship with God. Their need is to repent and turn again to their previous state of communion.

Sadly, because the Jews rejected the gospel of the kingdom time and time again, Paul and the other apostles turned their focus to the Gentiles and their spiritual needs.

In Rom. 11, Paul prophesied that Israel would remain blind to spiritual truth throughout the church age, *until the fullness of the Gentiles be come in*. Nevertheless, Israel will one day embrace Messiah and repent of national sinfulness. During the tribulation, 144,000 Jewish young men, chosen and protected by God, will evangelize their Jewish brethren, pointing them to faith in Jesus. But they will also preach the gospel of the kingdom. Jesus said, *And this gospel of the kingdom shall be preached in all the world for a witness unto all nations; and then shall the end come*, Matt. 24:14. Why will the gospel of the kingdom be preached during the tribulation? In order that the Jewish nation might repent and be restored as the wife of Jehovah to rule over the nations of the earth. Will Israel repent? The answer is found in Zechariah's prophecy.

> They shall look upon me whom they have pierced, and they shall mourn for him, as one mourneth for his only son, and shall be in bitterness for him, as one that is in bitterness for his firstborn. Zech. 12:10

How does the parable of the fig tree apply to Christians? Just as Israel needed to repent and become restored to fellowship with God to avoid temporal destruction and to inherit a place in the heavenly ruling realm of the kingdom, so church-age Christians need to repent and get right with God to avoid disinheritance at the Judgment Seat. *For whosoever will save his life shall lose it*, Matt. 16:25. That is, whoever lives for self now, will lose his reward at the Judgment Seat. Interestingly, the word *lose* in Matt. 16:25 is the same Greek word translated *perish* in our text in Luke 13:3, *Except ye repent, ye shall all likewise perish*. You, dear Christian, will *lose* your reward at the Judgment Seat if you live for self now. Consequently, any prospect of ruling and reigning with Jesus in the kingdom will be forfeited. Of course, you will regret that throughout eternity. Are you preparing to meet Jesus by walking together with Him in sweet communion?

Chapter 9

Speechless at the Judgment Seat

Parables of the Marriage Feast and the Husbandmen
Matt. 22:1-14, Matt. 21:33-40

Once again we have a parable before us that many in the evangelical world tend to *gospelize*, interpreting it as an illustration of salvation from eternal condemnation. But is that correct?

> 1 And Jesus answered and spake unto them again by parables, and said,
> 2 The kingdom of heaven is like unto a certain king, which made a marriage for his son,
> 3 And sent forth his servants to call them that were bidden to the wedding: and they would not come.
> 4 Again, he sent forth other servants, saying, Tell them which are bidden, Behold, I have prepared my dinner: my oxen and my fatlings are killed, and all things are ready: come unto the marriage.
> 5 But they made light of it, and went their ways, one to his farm, another to his merchandise:
> 6 And the remnant took his servants, and entreated them spitefully, and slew them.
> 7 But when the king heard thereof, he was wroth: and he sent forth his armies, and destroyed those murderers, and burned up their city.
> 8 Then saith he to his servants, The wedding is ready, but they which were bidden were not worthy.

9 Go ye therefore into the highways, and as many as ye shall find, bid to the marriage.

10 So those servants went out into the highways, and gathered together all as many as they found, both bad and good: and the wedding was furnished with guests.

11 And when the king came in to see the guests, he saw there a man which had not on a wedding garment:

12 And he saith unto him, Friend, how camest thou in hither not having a wedding garment? And he was speechless.

13 Then said the king to the servants, Bind him hand and foot, and take him away, and cast him into outer darkness; there shall be weeping and gnashing of teeth.

14 For many are called, but few are chosen. Matt. 22:1-14

Is this parable about salvation? Those who say it is interpret the invitation of the king as the gospel of grace by faith alone. Acceptance is receiving the gospel and becoming a possessor of eternal life and an automatic inheritor of the kingdom of heaven, which is Heaven, or eternal life. They assume that attendance at the marriage supper is for all saints. Rejection of the king's invitation illustrates rejection of the gospel of grace, with the ultimate result being cast into the lake of fire, which is represented by the term "outer darkness." Weeping and gnashing of teeth, they say, is suffering in the flames of eternal torment.

However, this interpretation completely ignores the context, not only the immediate context, but also the context of the book of Matthew and the Synoptic Gospels. Furthermore, it is based on theological assumptions that are forced upon the text. It is important to nail down from the start that the phrase *kingdom of heaven* is not a synonym for Heaven, the dwelling place of God and the assumed eternal dwelling place for saints.

The kingdom of heaven is literally translated "the kingdom of the heavens" and is referring to the ruling realm of the coming kingdom, the heavenly New Jerusalem. It will be the dwelling place of Jesus, along with His bride, where they will rule together, as regent and co-regent, over Earth. The other realm of the Messianic kingdom will be on Earth and is referred to as *the outer darkness*, or the darkness outside. It is called that because the kingdom of the heavens will be intensely bright, since Christ is the light thereof. In contrast, the earth will be dark, relative to the heavenly realm. Those saints who are consigned to the darkness outside, the earthly realm of the kingdom, will have resurrected bodies, but they will not be glorified rulers. In fact, for those consigned to the earthly realm, there will be great shame and restricted freedoms in contrast to the rulers who will have the ability to do marvelous things and go many places.

In this parable we learn more about the qualifications for inheriting the heavenly realm. Notice how the parable begins in v. 2, *The kingdom of heaven is like.* Jesus is going to tell us about some aspect of the kingdom and, as usual, it has to do with *reward*.

Invitation of the King

A king is preparing for the marriage of his son. Virtually all commentators identify the King as God the Father and His Son as Jesus Christ, and I would agree. From the parallel text in Luke 14:24, we learn that this wedding is the wedding *supper*, or feast, which is held at the start of the Messianic kingdom. It is the Marriage Supper of the Lamb in Rev. 19, which inaugurates the millennial kingdom.

In v. 3 the king sends out servants to invite folks to come to the marriage supper. As we shall see, marriage to Jesus and celebration with Him at the marriage feast are the *reward* of eternal life, not the *gift* of eternal life. In other words, this banquet is only for those saints who are rewarded at the Judgment Seat. Accordingly, this is not an invitation for the lost to be saved by faith. If it were, then Jesus and John the Baptist would have been preaching, "Believe on Jesus Christ and you will receive eternal life." But that is not the message they have been preaching here in Matthew's Gospel. What have they been preaching? *Repent, for the kingdom of the heavens is at hand*, which is not a salvation message.

Jesus is beseeching saved Jews to get right with God and follow Him in discipleship. That particular invitation is the context of this parable and the context of the book of Matthew, going all the way back to ch. 3. Those who accept Christ's invitation to discipleship will be included in the marriage supper. Those who do not will be excluded from the feast, for they will be excluded from the castle, so to speak.

They Would Not Come

What happens? Do the Jewish people repent and follow the Lord? The answer to that question is tragic, for v.3 says, *They would not come*. Putting it in parabolic form, the Jewish nation would not respond to the invitation to be wed to Jesus and thereby inherit the heavenly ruling realm of His kingdom. Despite their rejection, God graciously sends out more servants — see v. 4. Isn't our Lord gracious and merciful?

In the parallel passage in Luke 14, the people make ridiculous excuses as to why they will not come.

> The first said unto him, I have bought a piece of ground, and I must needs go and see it: I pray thee have me excused. And another said, I have bought five yoke of oxen, and I go to prove them: I pray thee have me excused. And another said, I have married a wife, and therefore I cannot come. Luke 14:18-20

Their outlandish response is summed up in Matt. 22:5-6, *But they made light of it, and went their ways … and the remnant took his servants, and entreated them spitefully, and slew them.* The remnant — a reference, no doubt, to the Jewish leadership — killed Jesus and later Stephen, and they persecuted the apostles. Jesus illustrates the depths of their depravity in the parable preceding this one.

"They Will Reverence My Son"

> 33 Hear another parable: There was a certain householder, which planted a vineyard, and hedged it round about, and digged a winepress in it, and built a tower, and let it out to husbandmen, and went into a far country:
> 34 And when the time of the fruit drew near, he sent his servants to the husbandmen, that they might receive the fruits of it.
> 35 And the husbandmen took his servants, and beat one, and killed another, and stoned another.
> 36 Again, he sent other servants more than the first: and they did unto them likewise.
> 37 But last of all he sent unto them his son, saying, They will reverence my son.
> 38 But when the husbandmen saw the son, they said among themselves, This is the heir; come, let us kill him, and let us seize on his inheritance.
> 39 And they caught him, and cast him out of the vineyard, and slew him. Matt. 21:33-39

A householder plants a vineyard and gives the custodial care of it to husbandmen, that is, keepers of the vineyard. At harvest time, the householder sends his servants to gather up the fruit. But the vineyard keepers beat one of the servants and kill the others. So the householder sends more servants. The vineyard keepers do the same to them. Finally, the householder sends his son, thinking, *They will reverence my son.* But when the son comes, the vineyard keepers kill him too! This prompts Jesus to ask a question of His audience.

40 When the lord therefore of the vineyard cometh, what will he do unto those husbandmen?
41 They say unto him, He will miserably destroy those wicked men, and will let out his vineyard unto other husbandmen, which shall render him the fruits in their seasons. Matt. 21:40-41

Although the Jews had not yet killed Jesus, His death was forthcoming. In fact, the handwriting was on the wall. For back in ch. 12 the Jewish leadership had rejected Christ's message of repentance, going so far as accusing Him of casting out demons in the name of Satan. That was blasphemy; they committed the unpardonable sin. So Jesus pronounces a terrible judgment upon the nation.

42 Jesus saith unto them, Did ye never read in the scriptures, The stone which the builders rejected, the same is become the head of the corner: this is the Lord's doing, and it is marvellous in our eyes? 43 Therefore say I unto you, The kingdom of God shall be taken from you, and given to a nation bringing forth the fruits thereof. Matt. 21:42-43

It is at this point that the offer of inheritance in the kingdom of the heavens is taken off the table for Israel and given to the church. Israel will receive inheritance in the earthly realm of the kingdom, for that had been promised repeatedly in the Old Testament, but the nation will have no inheritance in the heavenly realm, New Jerusalem, the heavenly city of reward. Individual Jews will certainly be included in the kingdom of the heavens if they qualify, but the nation as an entity forfeited the inheritance privilege. See Matt. 8:11-12, where individual, faithful Jews — for example, Abraham, Isaac, and Jacob — are rewarded as inheritors, while others from Israel are excluded.

The Kingdom Offered to the Church

Incidentally, the offer of inheritance in the kingdom of the heavens is also an *offer* — an invitation — to the church. Ruling with Jesus is not automatic. The offer must be accepted. What is the offer? Many think it is, "Believe on the Lord Jesus Christ and be saved." But that is not correct, for it is not contextual. As we have already pointed out, the offer is if saints will repent of their sinful lifestyle, and follow Jesus obediently in discipleship, then they will be included in the heavenly realm of the kingdom. All others will be excluded.

As a result of rejecting Christ's offer of inclusion in the kingdom of the heavens, not only was the offer removed from the table for national Israel, but something much more severe happened. *When the king heard thereof, he was wroth: and he sent forth his armies, and destroyed those murderers, and burned up their city*, Matt. 22:7. This is actually a prophecy, put in parabolic form. Indeed, John the Baptist had predicted in Matt. 3 this would happen if the people refused to repent. He said the axe would be laid to the root of the tree. That was a prophetic reference to the utter destruction of Jerusalem and the nation of Israel in AD 70 at the hand of the Romans. From our historical vantage point, this has already occurred.

Seeing the Jewish leadership rejected God's invitation, it was taken from Israel and given to the church. God is now making the same offer to church age saints that He made to Jewish saints in the past. That is the meaning of vs. 8-9 in the parable. *Then saith he to his servants, The wedding is ready, but they which were bidden were not worthy. Go ye therefore into the highways, and as many as ye shall find, bid to the marriage.*

The highways are a reference to the Gentiles, which predominantly comprise the church of Jesus Christ. While Gentiles would also receive the *gospel of grace*, that is not what is referenced here in v. 9. Being *bid to the marriage* means that Gentiles are also being given the opportunity to qualify to rule with Jesus in the heavenly New Jerusalem. Indeed, we know the apostle Paul taught the *gospel of the kingdom* to Gentiles as well, and so did Peter and the other apostles, according to the epistles. The offer is still on the table today. But the offer will soon be withdrawn, as the return of Jesus draws nigh.

> So those servants went out into the highways, and gathered together all as many as they found, both bad and good: and the wedding was furnished with guests. Matt. 22:10

What does it mean, *both bad and good*? Some say it means Jews and Gentiles, but that doesn't seem to fit the context, for the servants are now inviting out in the highways, which is Gentile in nature. Rather, this seems to be a reference to two types of saints. The Jews tended to look at people as either wicked and sinners (publicans and harlots) or religious and righteous (scribes and Pharisees). Jesus is using language they would understand. He is saying, compel both the publicans and harlots (saints living in vice-like outward habits) and the scribes and Pharisees (self-righteous saints) to come to my marriage feast. In fact, this interpretation is consistent with the parable of the two sons that we examined in the previous chapter (see Matt. 21:28-32).

God (represented by the king) wants His servants to reach out, not only to "bad" saints, who know they are not living right, but also to "good" saints, that is, religious, self-righteous saints who think they are spiritually okay. Could the latter group be referring to those Christians who think they don't need to qualify to rule with Jesus? Rather, they think that inheritance in the kingdom is automatic for all saints. Perhaps they are living legalistically, keeping a list, and maybe living hypocritically. They are outwardly obedient, but not necessarily inwardly. Both groups desperately need to hear the *gospel of the kingdom*, the invitation to inherit the kingdom. Those saints — bad or good — who accept the invitation and follow Jesus in discipleship will be at the marriage feast.

The wedding is finally filled with those who accept the king's invitation to rule with Him. They are predominantly Gentiles of the church age who have accepted the invitation of the King. But a man shows up at the wedding feast who is not properly attired. His offense is not wearing the appropriate wedding garment.

A Proper Wedding Garment

Those who *gospelize* this parable say the wedding garment represents the imputed righteousness of Christ. Therefore, since the man does not have Christ's positional righteousness, he is removed from the feast because he is actually unsaved. They would argue that saved people live and act like it, and thus the impartation of robes of righteousness must, of necessity, accompany any persevering saint. Those who have not persevered in righteousness are not true saints and will not stand before Christ at the Judgment Seat, much less be present at the Marriage Supper, they would claim.

Is that what Jesus is teaching in this parable? Not at all! The fact that this man is at the wedding feast means he is saved — not to mention that the king calls him "friend" in v. 12. This man represents those who think they are unconditionally the bride of Christ by nature of being saved. They expect to be automatic inheritors of the kingdom.

Unfortunately, this misconception was prevalent in Israel and is widespread in modern Christianity as well. In fact, multitudes of evangelical Christians think this way. Nevertheless, Jesus exposes the error of this thinking.

The King asks the man, *Friend, how camest thou in hither not having a wedding garment?* The man is speechless, for he thinks his garment is acceptable. He can say nothing; he has no adequate response. Again, this is not a lost man, waking up to the fact that he doesn't belong in Heaven. This is a saved man, waking up to the reality that he is unworthy to be part of the bride. I believe this scene is reminiscent of the Judgment Seat of Christ, when some are saved, yet so as by fire, and will undoubtedly have nothing to say for themselves.

Some may wonder, "Don't all saints receive white robes of righteousness that can be worn as the wedding garment?" God answers that question unequivocally in the book of Revelation when describing the Marriage Supper of the Lamb.

> Let us be glad and rejoice, and give honour to him: for the marriage of the Lamb is come, and his wife hath made herself ready. And to her was granted that she should be arrayed in fine linen, clean and white: for the fine linen is the righteousness of saints. And he saith unto me, Write, Blessed are they which are called unto the marriage supper of the Lamb. And he saith unto me, These are the true sayings of God. Rev. 19:7-9

The wedding garment that is required for attendance at the wedding is linen, clean and white — a garment that is pure and untainted. The temptation is to think we automatically possess such garments because of our position in Christ. After all, we have been justified, which means we have been declared righteous. However — and this is critically important to understand — the pure, untainted garments are not granted to saints based on our *position* in Christ, i.e., the imputed righteousness of Christ. According to v. 8, the garments are granted contingent on the righteousness *of saints.*

Making Your Own Robe

Interestingly, in the Greek, the word *righteousness* is plural. Literally, the fine linen garment is the *righteousnesses* of the saints — referring to the righteous *acts* of saints. Indeed, the garment *itself* is comprised of the righteousness acts of saints, not the righteousness of Christ. This means the garment is not based on your position in Christ (justification); it is based on your practical behavioral choices (sanctification). Putting it frankly, your lifestyle choices here and now are determining the type of garment you will be given at the Judgment Seat. You are making your own wedding garment by how you live here and now!

> Thou hast a few names even in Sardis which have not defiled their garments; and they shall walk with me in white: for they are worthy. He that overcometh, the same shall be clothed in white raiment. Rev. 3:4-5a

Clean, white, pure linen — which is the *only* acceptable wedding garment — will be granted only if you live righteously. If you choose to live for yourself, unfaithful to Christ, you will not receive righteous garments at the Judgment Seat. Your garments will be sullied.

Some tend to discount this view of Matt. 22 and Rev. 19 by interpreting what happens to the improperly dressed wedding guest as being cast into Hell. But does the Bible say he is cast into Hell? No, the king's verdict is, *Bind him hand and foot, and take him away, and cast him into outer darkness; there shall be weeping and gnashing of teeth.* Many *assume* outer darkness is Hell, but it is not.

The Consequences of Having the Wrong Garment

It is important to correctly understand the meaning of these statements.

First, *Bind him hand and foot.* Remember, this is a parable, a metaphor. The binding is not literal; it represents something. With respect to an unfaithful Christian who does not inherit the heavenly ruling realm of the kingdom, the binding of hand and foot clearly indicates a loss of freedoms. This saint will not be able to move about as freely as he would like in the kingdom. He will be greatly restricted and constrained in opportunities. Thus, the first recompense is loss of freedom.

Second, *Take him away and cast him into outer darkness.* The word *cast* may sound violent to some, but it need not. The same Greek word is used in Matt. 9:38, where Jesus says, *Pray ye therefore the Lord of the harvest, that he will send forth* (cast out) *labourers into his harvest* — parenthesis added. In Mark 1:43, after Jesus healed the leper, *He straitly charged him, and forth-with sent him away* (cast him out) — parenthesis added. The word *cast* is simply the idea of thrusting forth. Violence is not implied.

"But this man is being cast into outer darkness!" someone might object, "Isn't that Hell?" Regrettably, *outer darkness* has been misinterpreted by so many for so long that most tend to think it is a metaphor for Hell. But is it? Or is that view simply a theological hijacking of Scripture interpretation?

Why would a saint be cast into Hell? Why would someone Jesus calls *friend* be thrown into the lake of fire? The fact is, the man in the parable is *not* thrown into Hell! It is critical to understand that the term *outer darkness* simply means "the darkness outside." It is not a reference to Hell. In fact, the term is used three times in the New Testament and not once does it refer to Hell. To what, then, does it refer?

Marriage feasts would typically be held at night, so that one cast outside would be in relative darkness compared with the brightness of the banquet hall. But once again it is impor-tant to remember: This is a parable, a metaphor. "The dark-ness outside" is not a Hell-like place of torment. It is a realm of the kingdom. Charles Stanley correctly says, "To be in the 'outer darkness' is to be in the kingdom of God but outside the circle of men and women whose faithfulness on this earth earned them a special rank or position of authority."[5]

The man in the parable wearing the inappropriate wedding garment represents a child of God who longs to be at the marriage festivities with the bridegroom, for it is beautiful, and it is full of blessing. But he does not qualify to be there. He is thrust outside. The imagery used implies that he longs to be inside the bright and beautiful banquet hall rather than outside in comparative darkness. Furthermore, he longs for freedom, rather than being restricted in his activities.

How does he respond to the loss of inheritance? By *weeping and gnashing of teeth*, v. 13. He sorrows and agonizes over his foolishness, consciously regretting it. He is ashamed and full of remorse, grieved that he did not live for Jesus during his life. Undoubtedly, this is what John is warning against in 1 John 2:28, *And now, little children, abide in him; that, when he shall appear, we may have confidence, and not be ashamed before him at his coming.* God wants us to have boldness in the day of judgment (1 John 4:17)

The parable closes with haunting words, *Many are called, but few are chosen*, v. 14. In the context of the parable, this means multitudes of believers are invited to attend the wedding feast, but few of the saved will accept the invitation and be deemed worthy of ruling and reigning with Christ in His kingdom. What a sobering thought! Are you preparing to be chosen?

---

[5] Charles Stanley, *Eternal Security: Can You Be Sure?* (Nashville: Thomas Nelson Publ., 1990), p.126.

Chapter 10

Waiting for the Knock
at the Door

Parable of the Vigilant Butler
Luke 12:35-48

Years ago I attended a national conference for pastors. The conference theme was "Remaining Faithful." Tragically, faithfulness was repeatedly described by the various speakers as "grit-your-teeth" endurance in the fundamental doctrines of the faith and not giving in to the excesses of evangelicalism. That is a very shallow understanding of faithfulness. Little or nothing was said about the importance of enduring our sufferings as Jesus endured His sufferings. Hardly anything, if at all, was said about personally obeying the Lord and bearing fruit for His glory. Absolutely nothing was said about the importance of preparing for the kingdom because those attending the conference were of the mindset that all believers are overcomers, and therefore inheritors who will be rewarded in some degree at the Judgment Seat.

The biblical paradigm was wrong. The constant drumbeat from each of the conference speakers was, "Stick to it because the times are getting worse." In fact, 2 Tim. 3:1 was quoted several times during the course of the conference. There was no hope, no joy. There was no prospect of striving to become a son unto glory. It was simply, "Hang in there until the rapture, and then everything will be better." <u>A cloud of gloom hung over the place. It was one of the most miserable conferences I ever attended. Sadly, many churches beat the same drum week after week. Is it any wonder that millennials are dropping out of church in droves</u>?

We should rejoice that Jesus offers to us the privilege of ruling together with Him in His coming kingdom. To that end, we should also rejoice that He has given to each of us the provision to enable us to qualify. We don't have to trudge along in life merely "hanging in there." Every day with Jesus should be sweeter than the day before, as we grow in communion and fellowship with Him.

While we remain on Earth, we have an important and exciting mission for our Lord! Indeed, while He is away, we are His stewards, managing His household, and we should do so with great joy. Someone has said a steward is a person who owns nothing but is responsible for everything. When our Lord returns, He will recompense according to how we carry out our stewardship responsibility. To that end, in Luke 12 Jesus shares an intense parable about reward and loss at the Judgment Seat.

> 35 Let your loins be girded about, and your lights burning;
> 36 And ye yourselves like unto men that wait for their lord, when he will return from the wedding; that when he cometh and knocketh, they may open unto him immediately.
> 37 Blessed are those servants, whom the lord when he cometh shall find watching: verily I say unto you, that he shall gird himself, and make them to sit down to meat, and will come forth and serve them.
> 38 And if he shall come in the second watch, or come in the third watch, and find them so, blessed are those servants.
> 39 And this know, that if the goodman of the house had known what hour the thief would come, he would have watched, and not have suffered his house to be broken through.
> 40 Be ye therefore ready also: for the Son of man cometh at an hour when ye think not.
> 41 Then Peter said unto him, Lord, speakest thou this parable unto us, or even to all?
> 42 And the Lord said, Who then is that faithful and wise steward, whom his lord shall make ruler over his household, to give them their portion of meat in due season?

43 Blessed is that servant, whom his lord when he cometh shall find so doing.
44 Of a truth I say unto you, that he will make him ruler over all that he hath.
45 But and if that servant say in his heart, My lord delayeth his coming; and shall begin to beat the menservants and maidens, and to eat and drink, and to be drunken;
46 The lord of that servant will come in a day when he looketh not for him, and at an hour when he is not aware, and will cut him in sunder, and will appoint him his portion with the unbelievers.
47 And that servant, which knew his lord's will, and prepared not himself, neither did according to his will, shall be beaten with many stripes.
48 But he that knew not, and did commit things worthy of stripes, shall be beaten with few stripes. For unto whomsoever much is given, of him shall be much required: and to whom men have committed much, of him they will ask the more. Luke 12:35-48

Once again, Jesus shares a parable with His disciples (see vs. 1, 22, 32, 41), desiring to reveal truth to those who are ready and eager to receive it, while concealing truth about the kingdom from those who are blind and hard-hearted. By extension, He is speaking to saved people, and that includes saints throughout the church age. He wants saved people to progress in discipleship unto maturity, and that involves stewardship.

As children of God we are His servants by default. What kind of servant are you? We all want to be, as v. 42 says, a *faithful and wise steward*, whom our Lord will make ruler over His household. A steward is a butler, the one in charge of managing his master's affairs. In this chapter we are going to see another angle on what God considers faithfulness amongst His servants, and then we will discover four possible responses to stewardship.

What Characterizes Faithful and Wise Stewardship?

1. Vigilance

In v. 35 we are admonished to have our loins girded in a spiritual sense. Eph. 6:14 specifies our loins should be girded with truth, and 1 Peter 1:13 say the loins of the mind are to be girded up. What does this mean?

Jesus is drawing upon a common cultural illustration, involving the clothing of His day. In New Testament times most wore robes, typically long and flowing. While there may have been advantages in their culture to wearing robes, there was also a big disadvantage. It was difficult to run, or take strides, or work in the fields. To be able to function in activities of this nature, they would gird up their loins. One method of doing so was by gathering up the robe between the legs and either tying it or tucking it into the belt. This "girding up" would allow greater flexibility for movement, keeping one from getting tripped up.

In the Christian life, our thoughts can sometimes rage out of control and need to be brought into obedience to Christ (2 Cor. 10:5). This is illustrated by girding up the loins of the mind (1 Peter 1:13) and is referring to a disciple who is serious about truth and thinking correctly.

The other image used in v. 35 is having our lights burning, the opposite of being slothful and slumbering. Knowing that Jesus is coming again for His church, Paul admonished the Thessalonians:

> Ye are all the children of light, and the children of the day: we are not of the night, nor of darkness. Therefore let us not sleep, as do others; but let us watch and be sober. 1 Thess. 5:5-6

If your lights are burning, it means you are staying awake, alert, faithfully waiting for His return. Generally speaking, you are doing what the Master wants you to be doing while He is gone. In a spiritual sense, it means to be detached from Earth, not ashamed at the rapture, ready to meet Jesus at His Judgment Seat.

It's obvious that Jesus is speaking to saved people because he repeatedly refers to servants and their lord (master). Notice in each of the following verses the servant-master relationship:

> 42 that ... steward, whom his lord ...
> 43 that servant, whom his lord ...
> 45 that servant ... my lord
> 46 the lord of that servant
> 47 that servant ... his lord's will

In the parable, the *Lord* obviously represents Jesus Christ, and the *servant* is a saved person. <u>Unsaved people are never pictured as servants or awaiting their Lord's return</u>. That is only true of saved people. Christ is not the lord of unsaved people. But we are servants of Christ, by nature of our relationship as children of God, so this applies to us.

The return of Christ will come as a thief in the night for those who are not ready (v. 39). But for those who are faithfully awaiting His return, it is as if they are expecting a knock at the door (v. 36). Jesus promises blessing (v. 37) to those who are faithfully awaiting His return. They will be rewarded, but those who are not waiting will be recompensed in a negative sense. Thus, the first characteristic of a wise and faithful servant is vigilance.

The second characteristic of a faithful and wise steward is found in v. 42, as well as in the parallel text in Matthew's Gospel:

> Who then is a faithful and wise servant, whom his lord hath made ruler over his household, to **give them meat in due season**? Matt. 24:45 (emphasis added)

2. Teaching Meat (Not Merely Milk)

Not only is the faithful and wise Christian "butler" to be vigilant during the Master's absence, he is also to provide nourishing food (Gr., *trophe*) for those under his care. By using this particular word in the Greek, Jesus is emphasizing solid food in contradistinction to mere *milk*. The same Greek word is used in Heb. 5:

> 10 Called of God an high priest after the order of Melchisedec.
> 11 Of whom we have many things to say, and hard to be uttered, seeing ye are dull of hearing.
> 12 For when for the time ye ought to be teachers, ye have need that one teach you again which be the first principles of the oracles of God; and are become such as have need of milk, and not of **strong meat**.
> 13 For every one that useth milk is unskilful in the word of righteousness: for he is a babe.
> 14 But **strong meat belongeth to them that are of full age**, even those who by reason of use have their senses exercised to discern both good and evil.
> 6:1 Therefore leaving the principles of the doctrine of Christ, let us

go on unto perfection; not laying again the foundation of repentance from dead works, and of faith toward God. Heb. 5:10-6:1 (emphasis added)

The writer to the Hebrews wants those whom he is discipling to go on to perfection (v. 1); that is, he wants his audience to move on to maturity. He desires to transition his teaching from Christ's present high-priestly ministry, after the order of Aaron, to Christ's future ministry as a king-priest, after the order of Melchizedek. In other words, rather than continuing to focus his teaching on the cross — salvation by faith alone — and matters related to Christ's first coming, he wants to progress to the crown (reward) — salvation of the soul — and matters related to Christ's second coming.

Jesus will assume a Melchizedekian role when He ascends to His millennial throne. He is presently working toward the goal of bringing many sons unto glory (Heb. 2:10), saints who qualify to rule and reign with Him. But that subject is deep. It is meat-level truth, intended for those who are maturing. It is a mine of truth that needs to be dug out by serious saints.

Sadly, this truth is rejected by most Christians, who know virtually nothing about the millennial kingdom. So many are clueless as to the fact that we must *qualify* to rule with Jesus, assuming it is automatic. Why are so many ignorant of these truths? Because God's stewards are not faithfully teaching the meat of the Word. Bible preachers and teachers have settled for milk-level teaching. In fact, many have actually opposed meat-level teaching about the kingdom, in some cases even to the point of vehement resistance! As stewards, they are not giving meat in due season. If ever there was due season, this is it! We are on the very threshold of Christ's return. It is, therefore, urgent that Christians get prepared. Faithful and wise stewards are those who are teaching meat, not merely milk.

Although this applies primarily to pastors and teachers, it also applies to all saints, for we are *all* to be fulfilling the Great Commission (e.g., Matt. 28:19-20). Ironically, so many have made evangelism the focus of the Great Commission, whereas the biblical focus is on making disciples and teaching them to observe everything Jesus commanded. Disciples are those who are already saved and want to go on in their walk with Jesus. Are churches truly focused on making disciples, working to develop sons unto glory? Or is the focus mainly on evangelism? Of course, it all starts with evangelism, but for most churches evangelism is the end goal.

What a tragedy that so many newly saved people become members of shallow churches that are focused on milk rather than meat. What characterizes faithful and wise servants is that they teach meat, not merely milk, and they are vigilant about Christ's return.

We now come to four possible responses to stewardship. In other words, <u>here are four possible ways you can choose to live while awaiting Christ's return</u>. In fact, you are already responding to God, with respect to your stewardship, in one of these four ways.

Four Possible Responses to Your Stewardship Responsibility

(1.) Faithfulness

Notice again v. 42 in the text above where we find a faithful Christian. As a steward of Christ on Earth, he manages his affairs obediently. He serves God faithfully (i.e., full of faith). The faithful servant does not become consumed with the things of here and now. He does not look at the *things which are seen* but at the *things which are not seen,* 2 Cor. 4:18. His life is about seeking first the kingdom of God, Matt. 6:33. He bears fruit. He does not live unto himself, but unto Him who died for him. This Christian is a living sacrifice, holy, acceptable unto God. He has counted the cost and paid the price of discipleship.

What is the pronouncement of Jesus upon this child of God at the Judgment Seat? According to vs. 43-44, this servant is rewarded, for his works are deemed to be of the caliber of gold, silver, and precious stones (1 Cor. 3:11-15). He hears, *Well done, good and faithful servant.* He will rule and reign with Christ in His kingdom.

Unfortunately, there are three more possible responses to our stewardship relationship, and they are all negative, resulting in punishment, not reward. So let's look now at the second possible way you can choose to live while awaiting Christ's return and the corresponding judgment you should expect at the Judgment Seat of Christ.

(2.) Rebellion

In v. 45 we find a steward who mistreats those under his care and indulges himself. It is important to remember, this is a parable. The beating is not literal; it represents something. What are some possible ways a steward of Christ could be abusive to others?

Christian leaders could be guilty of "beating" by attacking faithful servants — those who are faithful in teaching truth about the kingdom, giving meat in due season. Sometimes pastors and Bible teachers focused exclusively on milk-level teaching (although no one admits to that) lash out against those who teach meat-level truth. This is a form of rebellion against God's truth.

Another form of rebellion is "indulging," for the verse speaks of the servant becoming drunk. Do you know any Christians who get drunk or abuse drugs? Do you know any Christians who live in adultery? Do you know any Christians who steal or lie or cheat or say horrible things? Do you know any Christians who yell at their family members? Do you know any Christians who have regular outbursts of anger? Do you know any Christians who are continually selfish, and because of it, they have destroyed their marriage or family? Do you know any Christians who live like the devil?

Why would any Christian do these things? Because in his heart he really doesn't take the return of Christ very seriously. He convinces himself, "My lord delays his coming," and so he is not vigilant, preparing to meet the Master.

Some have difficulty understanding how a true Christian could behave in this manner. "Surely," they think, "the rebellious servant is unsaved." To support this notion they assume these servants are four different people, the first one (the faithful servant) being truly saved, and the others being unbelievers. But they are all called *servants* in the parable, and as we noted earlier, the New Testament does not refer to unbelievers as servants. While Jesus expects His servants to be looking for His return and ready to give an account upon His return, He does not expect it of those who are unsaved. They are not His servants.

Furthermore, this is *one* person — one servant having four possible lifestyle choices — not four different servants. The term *that servant,* used in vs. 45, 46, 47, is the same as *that servant* in v. 43. In every case, it is the same individual. Jesus is showing what our outcome will be as servants, depending on the choices we make with our stewardship responsibility.

Cut Asunder?

Look at the dire consequences for the lifestyle chosen by the rebellious servant in v. 46. First, God will *cut him in sunder.* Again, we must keep in mind this is a parable. God doesn't literally hack His servant in pieces. Arndt and Gingrich say the Greek word translated here "cut asunder" is "metaphorical," meaning "to punish with utmost severity; like the modern threat 'I will tan your hide.'"[6]

This is a metaphor for the sword of the Spirit, which is the word of God, severely rebuking this rebellious servant. Rev. 19:15 says that from the mouth of the Lord Jesus comes a sharp sword. Consider also Heb. 4:12:

> For the word of God is quick, and powerful, and sharper than any twoedged sword, piercing even to the dividing asunder of soul and spirit, and of the joints and marrow, and is a discerner of the thoughts and intents of the heart. Heb. 4:12

I believe the first part of this punishment at the Judgment Seat is a strong, divine rebuke that reveals the inner core of this person by dividing between his spirit and soul and body. Why would God want to divide between the three parts of mankind? It is obviously not for His benefit, but for ours.

When you believed on the Lord Jesus Christ by faith alone for eternal life, He saved you. Technically, it was your spirit that was saved, forensically justified and made righteous by God. Your soul began to be saved and will continue to be saved throughout your Christian life, to the extent you cooperate with God as He works to sanctify you. However, it does not happen automatically. You must work together with God in the process (Phil. 2:12-13).

Many saints are not being sanctified, simply because they are not in cooperation with God. They have spurned His grace and continue to do so through repeated sinning. Oftentimes, this is spurred on by the erroneous thinking that since we are positionally righteous in Christ (which is true), we will face nothing of negative consequence at the Bema (which is false). In other words, there is a tendency for sinning saints to extend the righteous position we have in Christ within our spirit to the realm of the soul as well, thereby assuming the soul is also righteous by default, that is, by nature of our position in Christ. Nevertheless, this conclusion is dreadfully wrong.

If saved, we are eternally secure, regardless of the condition of our soul. However, the soul will be the focus at the Judgment Seat and will be recompensed accordingly. Perhaps this is the reason God divides asunder between soul and spirit — to expose the soul for what it really is. In that day you will not be able to hide behind your spirit and claim you are righteous (experientially) because your spirit is righteous (positionally). The soul — your mind, will, and emotions — will be laid bare in all its sinful ugliness. Undoubtedly, many saints will be horrified in that day of judgment, when they see the real condition of their soul apart from the righteous spirit. When that happens, no one will be able to say, "Because I am saved, I am an overcomer, an inheritor expecting reward." All will be revealed in the inner recesses of the soul. There will be shame and horror, shock and awe at the Judgment Seat

A Portion with Unbelievers?

The second part of the rebellious servant's punishment is found at the end of v. 46. God will *appoint him his portion with the unbelievers*. Because of this strong phrasing, many commentators have stumbled on this point and joined with the Calvinist interpretation (perhaps unwittingly), declaring this person to be unsaved. But that's poor interpretation of the parable.

We must be aware of two considerations. First, the word translated *unbelievers* here is often translated *faithless* in other places in the New Testament. So it doesn't have to mean an unsaved person. In fact, it can legitimately refer to an unbelieving Christian, one who is not depending on the Lord! For instance, when Jesus met Thomas in the upper room after His resurrection, Thomas doubted, prompting Jesus to use this very Greek word to describe Thomas.

> Then saith he to Thomas, Reach hither thy finger, and behold my hands; and reach hither thy hand, and thrust it into my side: and **be not faithless, but believing**. John 20:27 (emphasis added)

Thomas was obviously not an unsaved man needing to be saved. He was a saved man who needed to believe that Jesus had truly arisen. Jesus urged him not to be *faithless*.

In the context here in Luke 12, we must interpret this usage as an unbelieving Christian, that is, a Christian who is not depending on God for victory. He is faithless, like Thomas. He is living in defeat. I know many faithless Christians. They are saved and give a clear testimony of salvation by faith alone, but they are not trusting God to live a holy life. Thus, their life is displeasing to the Master, and they will be punished at the Judgment Seat. It is the opposite of the faith*ful* servant in v. 42. This one is faith*less*.

What does it mean, *appoint him his **portion** with the unbelievers* (faithless)? What is a *portion*? The same word is used in Luke 15:12 of the prodigal son, who asked his father, *Give me the portion of goods that falleth to me*. A portion is an allotment or share. Unlike the faith*ful* servant, whose portion is blessing and ruling and reigning with Christ, the portion of the faith*less* servant is no opportunity to rule or reign, and restricted freedoms in the millennial kingdom. Faithless servants will remain in the darkness outside.

According to the parallel passage in Matt. 24, this person's punishment prompts weeping and gnashing of teeth. Unfortunately, many Bible teachers have relegated that to Hell. But as spelled out earlier in this book, according to the oriental way of thinking, gnashing of teeth is simply conscious regret. That's all it means!

Imagine being harshly rebuked by Jesus at the Judgment Seat, not receiving any rewards, and having to live in eternity without an inheritance. If that is your verdict, you will weep and regret the fact that you did not live for God in this life. This is quite serious! You will reap consequences in the ages to come for how you live here and now. Perhaps you are re-lieved, thinking to yourself, "Whew! That doesn't apply to me. I don't live like this faithless servant." I certainly hope not, but it could apply to some who are reading this book. Live right-eously, for your Lord is coming!

We now direct our attention to the third possible way you can choose to live, while awaiting Christ's return, and the corresponding judgment you should expect at the Judgment Seat of Christ.

3. Indifference

What we find in v. 47 is a servant who knows His Lord's will but does not live accordingly. He may not be abusive or grossly indulgent as the rebellious servant, but he has an attitude of indifference nonetheless. Complacency has taken over the heart, and there is very little interest in spiritual matters. I personally think this servant's choices describe the vast majority of evangelicals who have at least a rudimentary knowledge of what God expects of His children. But multi-tudes of Christians have been taught in churches and Bible colleges that the Judgment Seat will be a few moments of emotional pain, then it will be over, and all will live happily-ever-after in the millennium. Not so!

Those who do not have an eternal focus will be *beaten with many stripes*. Again, this is a parable, and the stripes are figura-tive. Whatever form of recompense this takes at the Judgment Seat, we can't be sure, but it certainly doesn't sound pleasant. It is important to remember that whatever verdict Jesus gives at the Bema will remain with you throughout eternity.

Are you indifferent to your Lord's return? Are you living for yourself? Are you materialistic, maybe not compared to others, but compared to the Word of God? Are you bearing fruit for the Master? Have you left your first love? Do you have a form of godliness but deny the power thereof? What will be your verdict at the Bema?

We come now to the fourth possible way you can choose to live while awaiting Christ's return and the corresponding judgment you should expect at the Judgment Seat of Christ.

(4.) Ignorance

Verse 48 refers to those who do not know. They are ignorant of the consequences of living as a rebellious or indifferent servant. I cannot imagine this would apply to anyone reading this book because you have been warned. To whom much is given, much is required. In fact, I cannot imagine this last type of servant refers to evangelical Christians of the western world. We have access to Bibles and churches and open proclamation of truth. There is no excuse. We should live holy and righteous before the Lord.

If anything, I suppose this last group would be someone who was raised in a context where they had no access to biblical teaching. Perhaps it would apply to those in third world countries or pagan lands who get saved but have little opportunity for discipleship. Maybe they don't even have their own copy of the Bible. The Islamic world comes to mind. I cannot fathom that ignorance will be a valid excuse for western Christians at the Judgment Seat.

The parable of the vigilant butler boils down to this. All saints will give an account of their stewardship before the Lord and will be recompensed accordingly. Will you be rewarded at the Judgment Seat (in some degree), or will you be punished? If punished, do you realize what that could mean? It could result in forfeiture of millennial inheritance. It could mean you will not take possession of the eternal glories and blessings of the kingdom. Though you will be *in* the kingdom — in the earthly realm — you will not be an inheritor and will, therefore, miss out on the wonders of the heavenly realm of the kingdom. Your portion will be with the faithless. God intends for you to glow with the brightness of Christ, but you will not glow if you do not live for Him here and now. Are you a faithful and wise steward?

---

[6] BAG *Greek English Lexicon of the New Testament*, fourth edition (Chicago: Univ. of Chicago Press, 1967), 159.

Chapter 11

Ready to Meet the Bridegroom

Parable of the Ten Virgins
Matthew 25:1-13

The Olivet Discourse in Matt. 24-25 (cf. Mark 13; Luke 21) is Christ's teaching about the end times in response to His disciples' questions (see Matt. 24:3). Immediately following the doctrinal section, Matthew's Gospel records three parables shared by Jesus, illustrating the importance of preparing to inherit the kingdom of the heavens.

1) The vigilant butler, Matt 24:42-51, covered in the previous chapter,
2) The ten virgins, Matt. 25:1-13, to be covered in this chapter, and
3) The talents, Matt. 25:14-30, to be covered in the following chapter.

For First Century Jews or Church Age Saints?

Some Bible teachers claim the above three parables are exclusively Jewish in nature, having merely a passing ethical application for the church. However, this conclusion is unacceptable for at least four reasons.

1. While Jesus is speaking privately with His disciples (Matt. 24:3), who are admittedly Jewish, these disciples represent all future disciples of Christ that will follow, both Jew and Gentile. We know Jesus had future disciples in mind when instructing His initial men, for we see His heart in His prayer: John 17:20-21, *Neither pray I for these alone, but for them also which shall believe on me through their word; that they all may be one.* Furthermore, these same Jewish disciples became the foundation of the New Testament church (Eph. 2:20), comprised of both Jew and Gentile.

2. All three of these parables are about some aspect of the kingdom of the heavens. Yet, according to Matt. 21:43, Jesus took the kingdom of the heavens away from the Jews and gave it to another *nation* (Gr. *ethnos*) *bringing forth the fruits thereof.* The word *ethnos* is always used in the Scriptures to refer to the Gentiles, not the Jews. Thus, Jesus took the kingdom offer from the Jews and gave it to the predominantly Gentile church — particularly, to those who will bring forth the fruits thereof — that is, to those of the church who qualify.

3. According to Matt. 13, Jesus resorted to using parables for revealing truth about the kingdom to those who were ready and eager to receive it while concealing truth about the kingdom from those who were blind and hard-hearted. The Jewish leadership rejected the kingdom of the heavens offer of Jesus out of their prideful and hard hearts. So Jesus began speaking in parables for the benefit of those who would receive His teaching, predominantly the church.

4. Relegating these parables as exclusively for the Jews is meaningless when considering the gap of time between Christ's first and second coming as represented in these parables. In the parable of the vigilant butler, the servants of the Lord are to be faithful while the householder is away, and they will give an account when He returns. The parable of the ten virgins is about preparing to meet the bridegroom. He is presently gone, but will come to call out and reward His bride. The parable of the talents is about using God-given opportunities for His glory, while the Master is gone, with an accounting to come in the future.

The bottom line, each of these parables is about how Christ's disciples should behave while He is away — whether first century Jews or twenty-first century Gentiles — knowing they will give an account when He returns. These parables have nothing to do with Israel as a nation, for the nation had already forfeited its inheritance in the kingdom of the heavens. These parables are for saints of any era, whether believers of the church age preparing for the rapture, or tribulation saints awaiting the second coming of Christ. Either way, lifestyle choices must be made if one would qualify to inherit the kingdom of the heavens.

Gospelizing Tendency

Another interpretation mistake, often made by Bible teachers with respect to one or more of these parables, is to claim they are talking about matters of salvation from Hell. For instance, it is common to hear that five of the virgins were saved and five were unsaved. Even the revered Scofield Bible takes this mistaken position, thereby *gospelizing* the text. As already noted previously in this book, the parables are not soteriological. They have nothing to do with salvation from Hell. Parables are about matters of sanctification and discipleship. To say they are dealing with saved and unsaved is to do great hermeneutical damage to the Synoptic Gospels. We must rightly divide the Word of God, and that includes the parables.

As will become clearer as we go along, the parable of the ten virgins is about qualifying to be the bride of Christ, becoming His queen and co-regent in the millennial kingdom. That is a privilege conferred only upon those who qualify. It is not, as is widely taught, the expectation of every child of God. The bride of Christ is not comprised of the entire church but only that portion of the church that Jesus, the bridegroom, deems faithful and worthy to be His bride. Becoming the bride of Christ is equivalent to qualifying as a mature, first-born son or a son unto glory. It is conditional, not unconditional. All other Christians who are not deemed worthy of being Christ's bride will be consigned to another realm of millennial existence, the darkness outside. They will not participate in the Marriage Supper of the Lamb.

Debunking the "All-Saints-As-Bride" View

Before expositing the parable of the ten virgins, it is important to emphasize again a key passage in the New Testament that we examined in detail in Chapter 9. Unfortunately, it is often used as a support text for teaching that all saints compose the bride of Christ.

> Let us be glad and rejoice, and give honour to him: for the marriage of the Lamb is come, and his wife hath made herself ready. And to her was granted that she should be arrayed in fine linen, clean and white: for the fine linen is the righteousness of saints. And he saith unto me, Write, Blessed are they which are called unto the marriage supper of the Lamb. Rev. 19:7-9a

His wife hath made herself ready. These are the five prepared virgins who will receive the *fine linen, clean and white.* What is this fine linen garment? It is the *righteousness of saints.* As noted previously, the word *righteousness* is plural in Greek, thus referring to the righteous acts, or deeds, of the saints. This garment of white is the wedding gown, so to speak, but it is not given to all saints based on the imputed righteousness of Christ. It is given to those saints who *live* righteously (see Rev. 3:5a). Their righteous acts are their garment! Only those who receive the white linen garment will be included in the marriage. Others will be excluded.

Despite the clarity of this passage, many continue to assume that *all* saints will be part of the bride of Christ, but that is incorrect. For more on the bride of Christ, see my book, *The End of the Pilgrimage,* Chapter 9, "Prepare to Be the Bride."

The Marriage Metaphor

The parable of the vigilant butler, Matt. 24:42-51 — regarding our stewardship responsibility — is followed by the parable of the ten virgins, which shows how our stewardship responsibility affects our marriage to Christ. Once again, Jesus uses a parable to teach the qualifications for inheriting the heavenly realm of the Messianic kingdom and thereby becoming the bride and co-regent of Jesus. The moral of the story is clear: We must be prepared to meet the bridegroom or we will not be included as His bride.

1 Then shall the kingdom of heaven be likened unto ten virgins, which took their lamps, and went forth to meet the bridegroom.
2 And five of them were wise, and five were foolish.
3 They that were foolish took their lamps, and took no oil with them:
4 But the wise took oil in their vessels with their lamps.
5 While the bridegroom tarried, they all slumbered and slept.
6 And at midnight there was a cry made, Behold, the bridegroom cometh; go ye out to meet him.
7 Then all those virgins arose, and trimmed their lamps.
8 And the foolish said unto the wise, Give us of your oil; for our lamps are gone out.
9 But the wise answered, saying, Not so; lest there be not enough for us and you: but go ye rather to them that sell, and buy for yourselves.
10 And while they went to buy, the bridegroom came; and they that were ready went in with him to the marriage: and the door was shut.
11 Afterward came also the other virgins, saying, Lord, Lord, open to us.
12 But he answered and said, Verily I say unto you, I know you not.
13 Watch therefore, for ye know neither the day nor the hour wherein the Son of man cometh. Matt. 25:1-13

Keep in mind that parables are metaphors, using everyday situations to illustrate spiritual truths. Jesus uses the concept of Jewish virgins getting ready for marriage in their culture — according to their cultural way of doing things — to get across spiritual truth about the importance of preparing to become the bride of Christ. It is important that we not read our western cultural traditions regarding marriage into the passage. We must interpret according to the Jewish marriage customs prevalent during New Testament times. Following is a brief overview of the five stages of marriage in first century Israel (adapted from ISBE and other sources):

1. Betrothal. The groom-to-be would meet with the father of the bride-to-be and agree to marry his daughter. The result, if they could come to an agreement, was a legally binding marriage transaction. The couple was considered married at that point, but they continued to live apart, typically for a year, while the bride prepared for the wedding. The groom would go to prepare a home for his bride, usually as a room added to his father's house. This is what Jesus is presently doing for His bride, according to John 14:1-2.

> Let not your heart be troubled: ye believe in God, believe also in me. In my Father's house are many mansions: if *it were* not *so*, I would have told you. I go to prepare a place for you. John 14:1-2

2. Processional. The bride would be transferred from her father's house to the house of her new husband. This would typically happen at night in a torch-lit procession, involving guests. The bride did not know what day the groom would appear, so she had to be prepared for his arrival. A town crier would come by a little in advance to warn the bride of the groom's arrival.

3. Festivities. An entire week of feasting and celebrating with friends would typically precede the wedding ceremony, if any.

4. Ceremony. Oftentimes, but not always, an official wedding ceremony would be held toward the end of the week. Little details are available as to the nature of this ceremony.

5. Marriage Supper. The concluding event of the week was the actual marriage supper, after which the groom and his bride were ushered off to their new home to start their lives. It is important to keep this custom in mind when studying the parable.

The Kingdom of Heaven is Like ...

Jesus uses a marriage metaphor to teach His disciples about the kingdom of the heavens, that is, the ruling realm of the coming millennial kingdom. *Then shall the kingdom of heaven be likened unto ten virgins.* The moral of the story is, those who are ready and faithful at His return will be included as the bride and allowed to participate in the wedding festivities, including the marriage supper. Those who are unfaithful will be excluded from the celebrations.

As mentioned above, most Bible teachers would have us believe that this passage is referring to saved and unsaved. The five ready virgins are those who are saved, they say, and the five unprepared virgins are those who are unsaved. But that is a blatant abuse of the text. After all, they are all virgins. The unsaved are never compared to virgins, which refers to righteousness and purity. That image would be inappropriate for the lost. Furthermore, the apostle Paul said in 2 Cor. 11:2,

I have espoused you to one husband, that I may present you as a chaste virgin to Christ. He was speaking to saints at the church of Corinth.

The parable is simple. These virgins are preparing for the coming of the bridegroom. Keep in mind, they don't know when he will come. Since the bridegroom will come at night, they have lamps. The wise virgins have oil in their lamps; the foolish virgins do not. Incidentally, in the parable of the vigilant butler, we are admonished, *Let your loins be girded about, and your lights burning,* Luke 12:35. We are urged to be ready for the Master's coming and not be caught off-guard.

Ready or Not, He Is Coming

The point of this parable is that the wise virgins are prepared to be the bride while the foolish virgins are not. In light of the broader teaching of Jesus, the wise virgins are those saints who have renounced the self-life and have let go of worldly pleasures. They are fruit-bearing Christians. In contrast, the unfaithful are living for themselves, captivated by the world, indifferent to the Lord's return, not walking in the Spirit. They are not ready to meet Jesus, their life is not in order, and so they will be ashamed at His coming.

Since the hour is late, all of these virgins go to sleep. But they are awakened by the crier at midnight, who says, *Behold, the bridegroom cometh; go ye out to meet him,* v. 6. Notice the emphasis on readiness to meet the bridegroom — in our case, readiness to meet Jesus at the Judgment Seat. All ten virgins arise and trim their lamps to meet the bridegroom. The oil may represent the filling of the Holy Spirit.

Sadly, the foolish virgins don't have enough oil. As the end of v. 8 says, *Our lamps are gone out.* In the Greek, it is in the present tense, so it should actually read: "Our lamps are going out." They must go and buy more oil for their lamps. They are not ready to be the bride. The wise virgins cannot share any of their own oil, since every person will stand before Christ, accountable only for him or her self.

Why are the wise virgins considered wise? Because they have been living for Jesus. The foolish virgins are foolish because they have been living for self. While the foolish virgins are off trying to obtain more oil for their lamps, the bride-groom comes, and they miss the opportunity to become his bride. The door is shut, according to v. 10. What door is this? Is it the door to Heaven? No, Jesus is not talking about Heaven. He is talking about the kingdom of the heavens. He makes this clear in v. 1.

An open door represents remaining opportunity to pre-pare to be the bride. A closed door means there is no longer any opportunity to prepare; the time for judgment has come. This is obvious, for v. 10 speaks of the marriage, which is the marriage of Christ and His faithful church that precedes the launch of the Messianic kingdom. In particular, this is a reference to the marriage festivities, the supper that inau-gurates the millennium.

Jesus will be the king of the kingdom, and His bride will be the queen, so to speak. The queen will rule and reign with the king throughout the kingdom. That is why unfaithful saints are not included in the marriage festivities because they will not be ruling as Christ's bride (His consort queen) in the kingdom.

I Know You Not

What becomes of the unfaithful Christians, or we could say the five foolish virgins?

> Afterward came also the other virgins, saying, Lord, Lord, open to us. But he answered and said, Verily I say unto you, I know you not. Matt. 25:11-12

The statement of Christ in v. 12, *I know you not*, is quite strong. As mentioned earlier, it sounds much like the words of Jesus in Matt. 7:23, *I never knew you: depart from me, ye that work iniquity*. The particular Greek word translated *iniquity* in this verse actually means "lawlessness." It is referring to believers who are living disobediently. Thus, at the Judgment Seat, Jesus the righteous judge will declare, *I never knew you*, or, *I know you not*. This prompts many Bible teachers to conclude incorrectly that these five foolish virgins are unsaved. A pastor once said to me, "There's no way in the world Jesus would say, *I know you not*, to a believer!" Unfortunately, that pastor's response is based on his personal feelings rather than biblical truth.

It is important to interpret this strong statement in its context. The groom certainly knows these virgins, just as Jesus obviously knows all children of God. Indeed, being omniscient, He knows even unbelievers. Thus, the word *know* is unquestionably being used in a *relative* sense — relative to the context, which is worthiness to be the bride and inherit the kingdom.

Jesus does not know these virgins *as His bride*. Relative to the parable and the context, it means they are not fit to be His bride. They are not related to Jesus in a bridal sense because of their misbehavior. And so they are not allowed entrance to the marriage supper, for they do not qualify to enter the banquet hall.

Prepare to Meet Jesus

On the heels of the "I know you not" pronouncement, Jesus gives the moral of the story for all saints. *Watch therefore, for ye know neither the day nor the hour wherein the Son of man cometh*, v. 13. We all need to be preparing to meet Jesus at the Judgment Seat. An insightful commentator gives his conclusion to this parable:

> Most of us don't want to hear that we are expected to buffet our bodies, run the race, and through much tribulation enter into the kingdom reign. We would much rather hear that we will all inherit the kingdom, that we will all receive rewards, that we will all rule and reign with Christ, and that we will all attend both the wedding and the marriage supper of the Lamb. We want to hear that there are no consequences to a careless Christian life. Unfortunately, that's just not scriptural![7]

Thankfully, every child of God has been given equal opportunity to earn robes of righteousness because we have all been given the provision of Christ's righteousness. If you are appropriating His grace by faith (Rom. 5:2) to carry out His will on Earth, living a revived life, then you are a candidate for the wedding garment. However, for those who are ignoring this admonition, there are serious ramifications. You could miss out on the privilege of being His bride.

The hymn, *Are You Washed in the Blood*, appears in the "Salvation" section of our church's hymnal, but it is actually a sanctification song. The words speak to the preparedness that is necessary for inheriting the kingdom of the heavens.

> 1 Have you been to Jesus for the cleansing pow'r? Are you washed in the blood of the Lamb?
> Are you fully trusting in His grace this hour? Are you washed in the blood of the Lamb?
>
> 2 Are you walking daily by the Savior's side? Are you washed in the blood of the Lamb?
> Do you rest each moment in the Crucified? Are you washed in the blood of the Lamb?
>
> 3 When the Bridegroom cometh will your robes be white? Are you washed in the blood of the Lamb?
> Will your soul be ready for the mansions bright, And be washed in the blood of the Lamb?
>
> 4 Lay aside the garments that are stained with sin, And be washed in the blood of the Lamb;
> There's a fountain flowing for the soul unclean, Oh, be washed in the blood of the Lamb!

Rebuttal

I have taken the position in this chapter that the ten virgins collectively represent the church of Jesus Christ. The five prepared virgins become the bride of Christ, participate in the Marriage Supper of the Lamb, and rule together with Jesus in the heavenly Jerusalem, while the five unprepared virgins miss out on that privilege, remaining eternally secure, nonetheless.

Seeing this is a parable, the number ten is representative. In the Scriptures, ten is one of the numbers of completeness — Ten Commandments, ten plagues, ten toes and ten horns in Daniel and Revelation, ten generations from creation to the flood, etc. In the parable, I see the number ten representing the entire church of Jesus Christ.

Some commentators believe the virgins are bridal attendants or bridesmaids of a sort rather than the potential bride. Therefore, they conclude the virgins represent Jews of the tribulation period rather than the church of Jesus Christ. The prepared virgins are those Jews who become saved during the tribulation. They will be included in the marriage festivities as guests of the groom and His bride (which they take to be the entire church of Jesus Christ). However, this view is fraught with several problems.

First, why would a bridegroom come calling for bridesmaids rather than the bride herself? If the virgins are indeed bridesmaids, then the marriage imagery seems inappropriate.

Second, this parable is sandwiched between two others, the parable of the vigilant butler and the parable of the talents. Christ gives all three parables to His disciples — men who are already saved — to illustrate the importance of preparedness and watchfulness as stewards while the Master is away. The period of His absence cannot be interpreted as anything other than the church age.

Third, the Jews are not considered stewards in Christ's absence. Israel is in unbelief, having rejected the offer of inheritance in the kingdom of the heavens. That offer is now being made to the church.

For further explanation, please refer again to the beginning of this chapter, where additional detail is given. The big point to grasp is that while Christ is away, we need to prepare to become His bride, watching for and awaiting His return with great anticipation.

------

[7] Chuck and Nancy Missler, *The Kingdom, Power & Glory: The Overcomer's Handbook* (Coeur d'Alene, ID: The King's High Way Ministries, 2007), 136.

Chapter 12

Reward Positive or Negative?

Parables of the Talents and Pounds
Matthew 25:14-30; Luke 19:11-27

Imagine your boss at work entrusting to you a sum of money — or even his entire business — and asking you to manage his affairs wisely until his return. He doesn't know how long he will be away, but when he returns, you will be required to give an accounting. How will you manage the business?

Jesus uses a similar analogy in His parables of the talents and pounds.

> 14 For *the kingdom of heaven is* as a man travelling into a far country, who called his own servants, and delivered unto them his goods.
> 15 And unto one he gave five talents, to another two, and to another one; to every man according to his several ability; and straightway took his journey.
> 16 Then he that had received the five talents went and traded with the same, and made them other five talents.
> 17 And likewise he that had received two, he also gained other two.
> 18 But he that had received one went and digged in the earth, and hid his lord's money. Matt. 25:14-18

11 And as they heard these things, he added and spake a parable, because he was nigh to Jerusalem, and because they thought that the kingdom of God should immediately appear.
12 He said therefore, A certain nobleman went into a far country to receive for himself a kingdom, and to return.
13 And he called his ten servants, and delivered them ten pounds, and said unto them, Occupy till I come. Luke 19:11-13

The Nobleman on a Journey

Talents and pounds (minas) are monetary units, similar to dollars in our economy. In these parables a nobleman entrusts to his servants one of these sums of money and expects the servants to manage wisely in his absence. Interestingly, there is a common thread found, not only in these two parables, but also in the two others Jesus shares in Matt. 24-25, following the Olivet Discourse. The parables of the talents (Matt. 25:14-30) and pounds (Luke 19:11-27) feature a nobleman who is away on a journey and shows up unexpectedly. The parable of the ten virgins (Matt. 25:1-13) is about a bridegroom who returns unexpectedly for his bride. Finally, the parable of the vigilant butler (Matt. 24:42-51 and Luke 12:35-48) presents a householder who is away and shows up unexpectedly.

Why is the nobleman traveling on a journey? The Luke 19 passage says the man is going *to receive for himself* (that is, "to take") *a kingdom.* While he is away, the care of his estate is left in the hands of his servants. The application is obvious. Jesus does not intend to establish His kingdom immediately, that is, His millennial kingdom. He must first go and obtain it. He will be leaving His disciples and will be gone for quite some time. The period of His absence is obviously during the church age, between His first and second coming. As faithful servants, we must continue His business during His absence. All of these parables are about the importance of qualifying — as a faithful servant, a ready bride, a wise steward — to rule with Jesus, who is the householder and bridegroom and nobleman on a journey.

Taking the Kingdom

In what sense does Jesus need to *obtain* or *take* the kingdom? The answer to this question requires some explanation.

We know that Satan is presently the ruler of planet Earth. He wrested control of Earth's domain from Adam way back in the Garden of Eden. It's a long story, and we won't rehearse it all in this chapter. But suffice to say, that Jesus, through His death, burial and resurrection, earned the right to take dominion over Earth from Satan. Thus, in the book of Revelation we discover the *Lamb as it had been slain*, Rev. 5:6, taking a scroll out of the hand of God the Father. That scroll is the title deed to Earth, and, when opened, reveals the means by which Christ will retake the earth from Satan.

The book of Revelation — and for that matter, all of human history — culminates in 11:15, *The kingdoms of this world are become the kingdoms of our Lord, and of his Christ; and he shall reign for ever and ever.* That is the theme of the book of Revelation and the entire Bible. Christ will retake the kingdom of Earth and rule over it, bringing with Him selected *sons unto glory*, Heb. 2:10, who will make up His bride and co-regent to rule together with Him.

That is what Luke 19:12 is describing. Jesus is presently gone on a long journey, so to speak, working toward the goal of obtaining His kingdom. When He returns, those of the church that He deems faithful at the Bema seat will be rewarded as rulers. These parables are a metaphorical way of expressing how Jesus will reward His servants.

A Customized Stewardship Responsibility

Let's make this personal. *You* are God's servant. Jesus the nobleman is presently away, and He has left *you* with the responsibility of managing His affairs in His absence. *You* have been given a customized stewardship responsibility. A day of accounting is coming to determine how *you* carry out *your* stewardship responsibility.

Incidentally, this parable has nothing to do with investing money to get a good return on your investment. Jesus was not talking about matters of money. The parable merely uses a mundane monetary principle to illustrate spiritual truth. The point of the parable is that how we invest our lives spiritually determines the extent of our reward at the Judgment Seat.

It is also important to note up front that this parable has absolutely nothing to do with unsaved people. They are nowhere in question in this parable or any other parable, for that matter. As indicated throughout this book, parables are *not* soteriological. They do *not* deal with matters of salvation. Parables are for those who are already saved, urging us on with respect to discipleship and sanctification, with a view to the accounting we will give.

From the parables of the talents and pounds, we can learn four things.

1. God Assigns Stewardship Responsibility According to Ability

A talent is a unit of money, used only for illustration purposes in this parable. Notice in v. 15 that one servant is given five talents, another two, and another one. Every servant receives something, at least one talent, but more for some. The disparity is not unfair, for God determines every assignment, and each person is judged according to what God has given, not in comparison to others.

How does God determine the amount to give each servant? Verse 15 specifies, *to every man according to his several ability*, that is, to each according to his own ability. You have been given a stewardship responsibility based on what God knows is best for you. Our great God is all wise and compassionate and merciful, and so in the distribution of assignments, He is not seeking to burden you down so you cannot succeed.

Your stewardship assignment is according to your ability. That means according to your individual capacity. It is not a reference to natural abilities, but rather, what God knows is your spiritual capacity. Undoubtedly, there are many factors that contribute to your individual capacity. For example, when you were saved in the course of life, the unique opportunities for discipleship you have experienced, your personality, and other influences and factors God has brought your way, such as trials, chastisements, etc.

We cannot begin to understand how God determines what talent to give to each particular servant, but we can arrive at one conclusion from the parable. Everyone's stewardship responsibility will be different from everyone else's, according to what God determines. That is a very beautiful thing. But one thing is certain: To whom much is given, much is required (Luke 12:48).

I find it incredibly comforting that God has a unique expectation for each one of us that differs according to how He has built us. God made you, and He pre-determined what He wants you to accomplish for His glory. He will not hold *me* to your stewardship requirement, or vice versa. He will hold each of us to our own individual requirement, whatever He has customized according to our individual capacity. That is why one servant in the parable is given five talents, another two, and another one.

Did you notice in the parable of the pounds that each servant receives the same amount? Ten servants are each given a pound (mina), a different monetary unit than talents. Why is that? Ten is one of God's numbers of completeness, as we discussed in Chapter 10. The use of the number ten in this parable, for the ten servants — in like manner as the ten virgins in the previous parable — implies that *all* saints have a stewardship responsibility. Why are all given one pound, an equal amount? That leads to a second point.

2. God Expects Stewardship Compliance According to His Provision

The single pound given to each servant, I believe, represents the potential given to every believer in Jesus Christ when they are saved, the potential to live victoriously.

> Therefore we are buried with him by baptism into death: that like as Christ was raised up from the dead by the glory of the Father, even so we also should walk in newness of life.

> That the righteousness of the law might be fulfilled in us, who walk not after the flesh, but after the Spirit. Rom. 8:4

All believers have an "equal opportunity" provision to walk in newness of life, but many choose not to walk in newness of life. Tragically, while sin is powerless to rule saints, so many allow sin to continue ruling their lives.

> Knowing this, that our old man is crucified with *him*, that the body of sin might be destroyed, that henceforth we should not serve sin. For he that is dead is freed from sin. Rom. 6:6-7

The body of sin has been destroyed, that is, rendered inoperative. Because sin is powerless to rule, you don't have to yield to sin. You can live victoriously; you can yield to righteousness. What tremendous potential!

> Likewise reckon ye also yourselves to be dead indeed unto sin, but alive unto God through Jesus Christ our Lord. Let not sin therefore reign in your mortal body, that ye should obey it in the lusts thereof. Neither yield ye your members *as* instruments of unrighteousness unto sin: but yield yourselves unto God, as those that are alive from the dead, and your members *as* instruments of righteousness unto God. Rom. 6:11-13

When you are appropriating your God-given provision by faith (Rom. 5:2) and choosing to live righteously, you are living as a good steward, fulfilling your God-given potential. In this sense your pound can gain ten pounds and you will be rewarded accordingly at the Bema. That leads to a third point.

3. God Measures Stewardship Performance According to *Goodness* and *Faithfulness*

The nobleman returns after his long journey to reckon with his servants. Each servant is called upon to give an account to the master.

> 19 After a long time the lord of those servants cometh, and reckoneth with them.
> 20 And so he that had received five talents came and brought other five talents, saying, Lord, thou deliveredst unto me five talents: behold, I have gained beside them five talents more.
> 21 His lord said unto him, Well done, thou good and faithful servant: thou hast been faithful over a few things, I will make thee ruler over many things: enter thou into the joy of thy lord.
> 22 He also that had received two talents came and said, Lord, thou deliveredst unto me two talents: behold, I have gained two other talents beside them.
> 23 His lord said unto him, Well done, good and faithful servant; thou hast been faithful over a few things, I will make thee ruler over many things: enter thou into the joy of thy lord.

24 Then he which had received the one talent came and said, Lord, I knew thee that thou art an hard man, reaping where thou hast not sown, and gathering where thou hast not strawed:

25 And I was afraid, and went and hid thy talent in the earth: lo, there thou hast that is thine.

26 His lord answered and said unto him, Thou wicked and slothful servant, thou knewest that I reap where I sowed not, and gather where I have not strawed:

27 Thou oughtest therefore to have put my money to the exchangers, and then at my coming I should have received mine own with usury.

28 Take therefore the talent from him, and give it unto him which hath ten talents.

29 For unto every one that hath shall be given, and he shall have abundance: but from him that hath not shall be taken away even that which he hath.

30 And cast ye the unprofitable servant into outer darkness: there shall be weeping and gnashing of teeth. Matt. 25:19-30

Jesus will return to examine each one of His children to determine whether they have fulfilled their stewardship responsibilities while drawing upon His provision. What will Jesus expect at the Judgment Seat? Generally speaking, He will expect goodness and faithfulness. *Well done, thou* **good** *and* **faithful** *servant*, v. 21.

Good. A good saint is an obedient saint, one who walks in the Spirit as opposed to in the flesh, one who demonstrates uprightness of behavior and character, one who fulfills the law of Christ. This can only be accomplished through the power of the Holy Spirit. If you are good, it is not because of anything inherent in you, but because of God who has enabled you. Our Lord will determine if you are indeed *good* at the Judgment Seat, when all will be revealed. He will judge words and actions, thoughts and motives.

Faithful. *Moreover it is required in stewards, that a man be found faithful*, 1 Cor. 4:2. Technically, to be faithful is to be full of faith, carrying out your divine stewardship responsibility. But in a fuller sense, it is to be trustworthy and constant, continuing in your duty to God. It is steadfast loyalty to Him.

Aren't you glad that God is faithful? If He were not, we would be dead. Because of His trustworthiness we have life and can expect that He will fulfill His promises. The least we can do is to give Him our faithfulness.

4. God Rewards Stewardship Success or Failure According to Assignment, not According to a Universal Standard

Jesus is delighted that the servant given five talents returns five more (vs. 20-21). But He is equally delighted that the servant given two talents returns another two (vs. 22-23). He doesn't say to the man returning with two additional talents, "You have fallen short; the other guy before you brought five talents." No, thankfully, our God judges according to what He expects from each one of us and, as outlined in the first point above, He assigns stewardship responsibility according to ability. So you only need to return according to what God has given you. You never have to measure up to someone else's standard. In fact, there is no universal standard. I'm thankful for that because man likes to set universal standards — a sort of "one-size-fits-all." Men often judge churches, for example, as successful if they are large in size — big attendance.

No Universal Standard for Stewardship

Years ago I invited a guest preacher to speak in our church. Listening to him speak, I was horrified. He was talking about success in ministry, and he gave illustration after illustration of churches he considered successful because of size. He repeatedly mentioned numbers — the bigger the numbers, the greater the success, according to his philosophy. A really small church, in his opinion, was not successful. Now he didn't come right out and say it that way (he couldn't, for our church was quite small), but he implied it with every illustration. He also gauged success by how many "souls were being saved" week-by-week in the church and how many were being baptized. I wanted to raise my hand and ask the preacher what he thought about Christ's successfulness in ministry, seeing Jesus was rejected by a whole nation, and His "church" was comprised of only a dozen men. I also wanted to ask if he considered mega-church compromising pastors highly successful because they have such large congregations.

Here's my point: God doesn't judge in that manner, and for that we should be eternally grateful. Our Lord doesn't judge based on numbers, as man does. He doesn't have a universal standard for stewardship. The man who returns two talents in addition to his initial two (a one hundred percent return) hears the same commendation as the man who returns five in addition to his initial five (also a one hundred percent return). Why is that? Because stewardship is a very personal matter between Christ and His individual disciples based on every man's own ability. I love that! For it leaves judgment entirely in the hands of God.

Faithfulness Equates to Rulership

Notice the reward given. In both cases (five talents and two talents), Jesus says, *Thou hast been faithful over a few things, I will make thee ruler over many things*, vs. 21, 23. This could be paraphrased, "Seeing you have been trustworthy with some puny things that I entrusted to you, I will put you over matters of greatness and abundance." These two good and faithful servants, who have carried out their individual stewardship responsibilities according to God's expectations, are both rewarded with positions of ruling *over many things*.

The parable of the talents simply emphasizes that faithful servants are rewarded with rulership. However, in the parable of the pounds, the faithful stewards are told they will rule over a specific number of cities. In other words, different degrees of reward are given for faithfulness in that case. The one whose pound yields ten pounds (a one thousand percent return) will rule over ten cities, and the one whose pound yields five pounds (a five hundred percent return) will rule over five cities. That is because the starting amount for everyone is the same when it comes to Holy Spirit provision.

Thus, while the parable of the talents rewards according to ability, commensurate with the ability, the parable of the pounds rewards according to works accomplished in the power of the Holy Spirit, as opposed to works performed in the power of the flesh. Since all believers have the same provision — the same indwelling Holy Spirit — the reward is based on the extent to which the provision is accessed. That will vary greatly because not all saints choose to walk in the Spirit. Some will receive nothing, no reward, for they hide their talent or pound, walking in fleshliness.

For those who are rewarded, in addition to being given the privilege of ruling, Jesus says to them, *Enter thou into the joy of thy lord*, vs. 21, 23. In the context of the Synoptic Gospels, that surely means, "Come dwell together with me in the heavenly New Jerusalem, the kingdom of the heavens."

Negative Rewards

Those who are not good and faithful will not be allowed entrance into the heavenly New Jerusalem. They will not be rewarded with the privilege of ruling together with Jesus. On the contrary, they will receive a *negative* reward. This concept, for some reason, is foreign to the modern day church of Jesus Christ. According to the Scriptures, the prospect of negative reward at the Bema is real. Consider Col. 3:25a, *But he that doeth wrong shall receive for the wrong which he hath done*.

What is the reason given by the unfaithful servant as to why he does not produce works for the Master? Look at v. 24. His reply is astounding! What this unfaithful saint is essentially saying is that his Lord is unfair and selfish, for He reaps though He doesn't do any of the work of sowing. He benefits from the harvest, though He doesn't do any of the work of gathering in the crops. The servants do all the work, but don't reap the benefits of it. The Master is the only one to benefit.

How foolish! What this servant fails to realize is that while his statement is *technically* true, there is a reason for the Master's method. Jesus is giving His servants opportunities to prove themselves and to demonstrate faithfulness to Him. In the end, if they are faithful, they will be rewarded abundantly with eternal treasures!

Incidentally, ignorance of the Master's intentions with respect to rewarding His servants is characteristic of modern Christianity. So few pastors and Bible teachers are preparing their congregations to rule with Jesus. They assume rulership is automatic for all believers, that all will rule, that all saints are overcomers by nature of their saving faith. But that is completely wrong and unscriptural! Those who take this position are guilty of producing wicked and slothful servants. As a result, nothing of value is being accomplished for the Lord in the lives of many saints.

What are the negative rewards for non-productive saints?

1. Rebuke by Jesus. *Thou wicked and slothful servant*, v. 26 — the opposite of good and faithful. As part of this rebuke, Jesus says, "You should at least have returned a little interest on my money," v. 27.

2. Opportunity Taken Away. *Take therefore the talent from him, and give it unto him which hath ten talents*, v. 28. What had been initially given to this servant is taken away and given to the one having ten talents. The reason for this is explained in v. 29, *For unto every one that hath shall be given, and he shall have abundance: but from him that hath not shall be taken away even that which he hath.*

The reason the talent is given away is to demonstrate that the opportunity for reward is over. When the rapture occurs and the Judgment Seat begins, there is no longer an opportunity to be faithful as a steward. Taking the talent away from the servant is like the door closing on the five unprepared virgins in the previous parable.

3. Cast Into Outer Darkness. *Cast ye the unprofitable servant into outer darkness: there shall be weeping and gnashing of teeth*, v. 30. This scares some Christians, so they conclude it must be referring to the unsaved because they assume outer darkness is Hell. However, outer darkness is not Hell, and the servant in this parable cannot be unsaved. In v. 30 this unfaithful one is referred to as *the unprofitable **servant***. Unbelievers are never called servants. Furthermore, in v. 14 the nobleman calls his *own* servants. This is clearly a saved person — one of the master's *own* servants — who has been unprofitable to his Lord. The word *unprofitable* means "useless" and in this context implies that the saint has not borne any fruit.

What, then, is outer darkness? As we have already seen extensively in previous chapters, outer darkness is the relative darkness outside the New Jerusalem, which is extremely bright because Christ is the light thereof. It is the earthly realm of the millennial kingdom rather than the heavenly realm where Christ rules and reigns with His faithful disciples. Unprofitable servants will not have the privilege of ruling with Jesus in the multi-dimensional heavenly realm. In other words, they will have restricted freedoms. For this reason, they will weep and gnash their teeth, expressing grief and sorrow. Those in the darkness outside will be ashamed and will deeply regret how they lived while on Earth.

Incidentally, in the parable of the pounds in Luke 19, don't be confused by v. 27, *But those mine enemies, which would not that I should reign over them, bring hither, and slay them before me.* Who are these citizens? The answer is found in v. 14, *But his citizens hated him, and sent a message after him, saying, We will not have this man to reign over us.* The citizens represent the nation of Israel that incurred God's judgment in AD 70 because the national leaders spurned Christ's offer to rule together with Him in the heavenly New Jerusalem.

The *servants in both parables* (Matt. 25, Luke 19) represent the "other nation" to whom Jesus offers the kingdom of the heavens after Israel rejected it. The "other nation," of course, is the church of Jesus Christ, an entirely different entity, to whom the offer is presently being made. If you, as a servant of Jesus Christ in this church age, desire to rule with Jesus — and you should desire it — then you must qualify according to the terms of the parables. Indeed, every child of God ought to take the parable of the talents and the parable of the pounds with utmost sincerity. There is much at stake.

We will all give an account, individually, for our stewardship while the nobleman is away. If you were to stand before Jesus right this instant, would He say to you, *Well done, good and faithful servant,* or would He say, *Thou wicked and slothful servant?*

The final four chapters will present parables that teach us how to prepare to hear those precious words, *Well done!*

Chapter 13

Blessed Are the Merciful

Parable of the Unmerciful Servant
Matthew 18:23-35

Shakespeare frequently quoted the Bible and referred to biblical concepts. For instance, in his play, *The Merchant of Venice*, the Duke of Venice asks Shylock, "How shalt thou hope for mercy, rendering none?" That is a good question indeed, and one that Jesus answers in the parable of the unmerciful servant.

Not one of us deserves God's mercy, but He has bestowed mercy upon us by saving and forgiving us of all past, present, and future sin. We deserve justice, the lake of fire, but instead God graciously bestows mercy upon us every day of our Christian lives.

Knowing God has showered His mercy so overwhelmingly upon us, we ought to be merciful toward others. In fact, we will give an account one day as to whether we demonstrate mercy throughout our lives. If so, there will be reward; if not, there will be punishment (negative consequence). That is the point of the parable given by Jesus in Matt. 18.

23 Therefore is the kingdom of heaven likened unto a certain king, which would take account of his servants.

24 And when he had begun to reckon, one was brought unto him, which owed him ten thousand talents.

25 But forasmuch as he had not to pay, his lord commanded him to be sold, and his wife, and children, and all that he had, and payment to be made.

26 The servant therefore fell down, and worshipped him, saying, Lord, have patience with me, and I will pay thee all.

27 Then the lord of that servant was moved with compassion, and loosed him, and forgave him the debt.

28 But the same servant went out, and found one of his fellow-servants, which owed him an hundred pence: and he laid hands on him, and took him by the throat, saying, Pay me that thou owest.

29 And his fellowservant fell down at his feet, and besought him, saying, Have patience with me, and I will pay thee all.

30 And he would not: but went and cast him into prison, till he should pay the debt.

31 So when his fellowservants saw what was done, they were very sorry, and came and told unto their lord all that was done.

32 Then his lord, after that he had called him, said unto him, O thou wicked servant, I forgave thee all that debt, because thou desiredst me:

33 Shouldest not thou also have had compassion on thy fellow-servant, even as I had pity on thee?

34 And his lord was wroth, and delivered him to the tormentors, till he should pay all that was due unto him.

35 So likewise shall my heavenly Father do also unto you, if ye from your hearts forgive not every one his brother their trespasses. Matt. 18:23-35

A Requirement for Kingdom Inheritance

Notice how Jesus starts the parable: *The kingdom of heaven is likened unto*, v. 23. This parable relates in story form one of the requirements for inheriting the kingdom of the heavens. Once again, by *inheriting the kingdom* we are not referring to the matter of salvation from eternal condemnation. There is nothing anyone can do to earn salvation. Eternal life is given by God to those who depend on His Son Jesus Christ to save from sin.

Once you believe, your eternal destiny is secure; nothing can change it. You cannot lose or forfeit this aspect of salvation. However, you can forfeit the privilege of inheriting the kingdom, or we could say, ruling together with Jesus in His coming kingdom. That is a matter of reward according to works, and it is conditional. You must meet God's conditions to qualify. This parable gives one of the conditions. There are several other qualifications mentioned by Jesus, particularly in the Sermon on the Mount.

How do we know mercy is a requirement for inheriting the kingdom? Verse 23 speaks of a king taking account of his servants. That is a picture of each one us standing before our King at the Judgment Seat of Christ. As children of God we are His servants, and subject to accounting, based on how we live. The point of this parable is that those who show mercy will obtain mercy; those who do not show mercy will not receive mercy. Let's see how this unfolds in the parable.

Accounting to the King

A king decides to take account of his servants. The same Greek word translated *take account* in v. 23 is translated *reckon* in v. 24. It is the idea of computing — "doing the books," an accountant might say. In the course of his accounting, the king finds that one of his servants owes him ten thousand talents, a scandalous amount. The implication is that the servant has embezzled from the king, for this is an enormous sum of money. In fact, a talent is about 75 lbs. in weight. Ten thousand talents would be 750,000 lbs., probably of silver. If we multiply the 750,000 lbs. of silver by 16 to get the number of ounces, we arrive at 12 million ounces. At the time of writing, silver is trading at $17.00 per ounce. Doing more math, we arrive at a value of $204 million!

This servant has embezzled an astronomical amount from the king and now it is a debt owed, for he has been caught. The debt is impossible. There is no way the man can pay. As v. 25 indicates, the king commands that the man be sold into slavery, along with his wife and children, and all that he possesses be sold to pay off the debt. Obviously, this debt will *never* be repaid. It is far too great. In fact, one commentator says:

> Ten thousand (*myria*, hence our 'myriad') is the largest numeral for which a Greek term exists, and the talent is the largest known amount of money. When the two are combined, the effect is like our "zillions."[8]

This guy owes "zillions," we might say sarcastically, and there's no way he could repay it, even in a hundred lifetimes. So he falls down and worships the king, bowing and scraping and even kissing the king's hands or feet — this is actually implied in the Greek word used. He begs the king to be patient, for he will repay all. This is utterly ridiculous. In fact, it's not possible!

The Merciful King

This king is gracious, and he knows the man cannot pay his debt. But because the man is humble and contrite, the gracious king is moved with compassion, releases him from the debt and forgives the amount owed. It is as if the debt never existed.

Many commentators say the parable pictures salvation from eternal condemnation. But I don't believe that is the case, and I will explain why in just a moment. It is certainly true that when we were saved God forgave our impossible sin debt. In fact, He removed our sin — past, present, and future. Heb. 10:17, *Their sins and iniquities will I remember no more.* Hallelujah! What a wonderful standing we have in Christ! But this parable seems to be illustrating something else, something related to Christian living.

It is important to notice that the debtor is the king's servant from the very start of the parable. He doesn't start out a non-servant or unsaved man in v. 23 and then get saved and become a servant in v. 27, as so many commentators claim. He is called a servant from the start, and the word *servant* is never used of unbelievers in the New Testament. This is a saved man from the very beginning of the parable. What, then, is this accounting in v. 23 that leads to the man's contrite heart in v. 26 and God's forgiveness in v. 27?

Think about it, we sin practically every day of our lives. When we do, God shines a light on our sin through His Word and through Holy Spirit conviction, even using our conscience. That is an ongoing form of accounting that happens all throughout the Christian life and will culminate at the Judgment Seat. When we refuse to acknowledge our sin, even after God has exposed it, we are judged by God — yes, even in this life. It's called God's chastening or discipline, or even judgment — and we see that in v. 25.

Why are the wife and children also sold into slavery? Because our sin also affects our family and others around us, and so does God's discipline of us. For instance, if God allows one of us to become sick or lose our job specifically as chastening for resisting His will, then our family suffers also. But when we agree with God about our sin, confessing it in the spirit of 1 John 1:9, we are like the man in v. 26 bowing before the king with a contrite heart, asking for mercy.

How does God respond to those who humbly seek His mercy? He forgives sin and cleanses from all unrighteousness. The impossible sin debt that we bring to God every time we confess our sins — the sin debt that we could not possibly pay of ourselves — He forgives and cleanses. He is so merciful! We don't deserve forgiveness, but God forgives us on account of Jesus who lives within us. How many times throughout your Christian life have you sought God's forgiveness, and He has given it?

The Tables Are Turned

We now come to the point of the parable. The tables are now turned. The forgiven man discovers that one of his fellow servants owes him a hundred pence, or one hundred denarii. That's the equivalent of a hundred day's wages. In our economy, let's say a factory worker makes around $35,000 per year. This debt would be one hundred days' worth of that salary, or around $9,500. That's certainly not pocket change, but in comparison to the impossible debt that was forgiven the first man, it's a small amount.

The parable now turns ugly. Notice what the forgiven man does to his fellow servant. According to the end of v. 28, he cruelly insists on payment in full, choking the debtor. The fellow servant, having no present ability to pay, does the same thing that the forgiven man had done to the king. He falls down at the creditor's feet and begs for patience until he can repay the debt. Verse 30 is astounding! The creditor orders the debtor to be cast into prison. How can the fellow servant repay the debt if he is in prison? The implication is that this servant will be imprisoned indefinitely because of the forgiven man's lack of mercy.

What happens in the end? The other servants are so horrified at how the forgiven man has treated his fellow servant that they tell the king about it (v. 31). The king is astounded that the one to whom he has shown such great compassion and forgiven the impossible debt does not, in return, show similar kindness to another who owes a far smaller debt. The assumption is that one forgiven so much should be inclined to forgive others of lesser debts. The king seems heartbroken by his servant's merciless spirit toward others, particularly after he has been treated so mercifully.

> O thou wicked servant, I forgave thee all that debt, because thou desiredst me: Shouldest not thou also have had compassion on thy fellowservant, even as I had pity on thee? Matt. 18:32-33

Unmerciful Servants Are Punished

The king's heart of mercy, now spurned, turns to a heart of anger and justice. Notice what he does (v.34). He turns over the unmerciful servant to the tormentors until he pays the entire debt due to him. That prompts a question: Will the servant ever be able to pay that debt, even in a million years? No, for he is in prison, being tormented. His family is not with him now; he is on his own.

The moral of the story in found in v. 35, *So likewise shall my heavenly Father do also unto you, if ye from your hearts forgive not every one his brother their trespasses.*

This parable is about a Christian, a child of God like you. When you sin, but do not seek God's forgiveness, He chastens and may resort to judgment, if necessary, until you confess your sins. Once you confess, He forgives your impossible debt. But there's an exception. When you choose not to forgive others who have offended you, then God does not forgive *you*. Although you may not experience any repercussions in this life, you will at the Judgment Seat, and that is what v. 34 is all about, *His lord was wroth, and delivered him to the tormentors, till he should pay all that was due unto him.*

I remind you that this is a parable, a metaphor. God does not literally torment His children. But to what can we liken the torment spiritually? The torment cannot represent Hell, for the man is clearly saved. It seems to be a reference to the outer darkness. The unmerciful servant is tormented in the sense that he has forfeited the opportunity to live and dwell and rule with Jesus in the heavenly New Jerusalem. Rather, he is in the relative darkness outside, weeping and gnashing his teeth, consciously regretting his foolish choices while living on Earth. That is tormenting in the sense that the verdict cannot change.

The possibility of negative reward — we could even say *punishment* — at the Bema is a reality. None of us wants to experience that kind of verdict, and so we must, by the grace of God, avoid being unmerciful servants.

The Marks of an Unmerciful Heart

How can you determine if you are unmerciful? What characterizes an unmerciful heart?

1. An Unforgiving Spirit.

We clearly see this in the parable when the servant forgiven the impossible debt refuses to forgive the debt of a fellow servant who owes a small sum, comparatively. However, it is important not to miss the context of the parable, for Jesus addresses the matter of unforgiveness in advance of the parable. For instance, in vs. 15-17, our Lord gives a biblical protocol for dealing with offenses between brethren in the church. Then in v. 21 we find Peter's classic question: *Lord, how oft shall my brother sin against me, and I forgive him? till seven times?* Peter thought he was being generous, in light of Amos 2:6 which shows God being merciful and forgiving to Judah three times. Thus Peter, trying to demonstrate a magnanimous spirit, says, "Lord, should we forgive *seven* times?"

We are well acquainted with Christ's response: *I say not unto thee, until seven times: but, until seventy times seven*, Matt. 18:22. The Septuagint translates as *seventy-seven times*. Either way, we are to forgive repeatedly. Incidentally, doesn't God forgive *you* repeatedly — every time you ask — time after time again? He wants you to have that same spirit. Those who do not forgive others will not be forgiven by God, particularly at the Judgment Seat. They will be cast into the darkness outside rather than having the opportunity to rule with Jesus in His millennial kingdom.

The parable that follows in vs. 23-35 is simply an illustration of what Jesus had taught earlier in the chapter and, for that matter, even earlier in the Sermon on the Mount.

> Forgive us our debts, as we forgive our debtors ... For if ye forgive men their trespasses, your heavenly Father will also forgive you: But if ye forgive not men their trespasses, neither will your Father forgive your trespasses. Matt. 6:12, 14-15

No matter how much you invoke 1 John 1:9, God will *not* forgive your trespasses unless you forgive others for what they have done to you. Husband, forgive your wife. Wife, forgive your husband. Children forgive your parents. Parents, forgive your children. Christian, forgive your brothers and sisters in Christ. Why? Because God commands it. *Be ye kind one to another, tenderhearted, forgiving one another, even as God for Christ's sake hath forgiven you,* Eph. 4:32. There is a second way we can be unmerciful.

2. A Judgmental Spirit

> Judge not, that ye be not judged. For with what judgment ye judge, ye shall be judged: and with what measure ye mete, it shall be measured to you again. Matt. 7:1-2

Are you guilty of having a judgmental spirit toward other believers? If so, then God will use the same ruler of judgment you have used on others, for judging you. In other words, you will be measured in like manner as you have measured others. Constable shares some excellent thoughts on the meaning of this command.

> Jesus taught His disciples not to be judgmental or censorious (i.e., hypercritical, fault-finding, condemning) of one another, in view of the high standards He was clarifying (cf. Rom. 14:10- 13; James 4:11-12). He did not mean that they should accept everything and everyone uncritically (cf. vv. 5-6, 15-20; John 7:24; 1 Cor. 5:5; Gal. 1:8-9; 6:1; Phil. 3:2; 1 John 4:1). Neither did He mean, obviously, that parents, church leaders, and civil authorities are wrong if they pass judgment on those under their care. He meant that His

disciples should not do God's job of passing judgment—for Him—when He has not authorized them to do so. They really could not, since no one but God knows all the facts that motivate people to do as they do. The disciple who usurps God's place will have to answer to Him for doing so.[9]

Ouch! Hearing this is painful. We must not be unforgiving or judgmental. There is a third way we can be unmerciful.

3. A Condescending, Hypocritical Spirit

Why beholdest thou the mote that is in thy brother's eye, but considerest not the beam that is in thine own eye? Or how wilt thou say to thy brother, Let me pull out the mote out of thine eye; and, behold, a beam is in thine own eye? Thou hypocrite, first cast out the beam out of thine own eye; and then shalt thou see clearly to cast out the mote out of thy brother's eye. Matt. 7:3-5

How often do we see the glaring sins of others while not seeing our own? Worse yet, dismissing our own sins as "no big deal," while deeming the sins of others "a really big deal," is hypocritical and condescending, the sin of the Pharisees.

Consider the parallel text to Matt. 7:1-5 in Luke's Gospel, where Jesus adds another brief parable.

Judge not, and ye shall not be judged: condemn not, and ye shall not be condemned: forgive, and ye shall be forgiven: Give, and it shall be given unto you; good measure, pressed down, and shaken together, and running over, shall men give into your bosom. For with the same measure that ye mete withal it shall be measured to you again. **And he spake a parable unto them, Can the blind lead the blind? shall they not both fall into the ditch?** The disciple is not above his master: but every one that is perfect shall be as his master. And why beholdest thou the mote that is in thy brother's eye, but perceivest not the beam that is in thine own eye? Luke 6:37-41 (emphasis added)

Those who are unforgiving and judgmental and condemning are like the blind leading the blind: They will both fall into the ditch. Then Jesus adds something else:

For a good tree bringeth not forth corrupt fruit; neither doth a corrupt tree bring forth good fruit. For every tree is known by his own fruit. For of thorns men do not gather figs, nor of a bramble bush gather they grapes. A good man out of the good treasure of his heart bringeth forth that which is good; and an evil man out of

> the evil treasure of his heart bringeth forth that which is evil: for of
> the abundance of the heart his mouth speaketh. Luke 6:43-45

If you are unforgiving, judgmental, condemning, condescending and hypocritical, not only are you blind, but you are
inwardly corrupt, bringing forth corrupt fruit. You are unmerciful! No wonder that Jesus deals with His unmerciful
servants so severely. The consequences will be dire in the
coming judgment. Let's look at one more passage.

> And it came to pass, as Jesus sat at meat in the house, behold,
> many publicans and sinners came and sat down with him and his
> disciples. And when the Pharisees saw it, they said unto his
> disciples, Why eateth your Master with publicans and sinners?
> Matt. 9:10-11

Jesus has been preaching, *Repent, for the kingdom of the
heavens is at hand*, Matt. 4:17. Many publicans and sinners are
listening to His message, and many are getting right with
God, even submitting to John's baptism of repentance. But this
makes the Pharisees upset because they don't like Jesus eating
with these people. They think they are above Christ's call to
repentance, proclaiming, *We have Abraham to our father*, Matt.
3:9. Here's how Jesus responds to the Pharisees:

> But when Jesus heard that, he said unto them, They that be whole
> need not a physician, but they that are sick. Matt. 9:12

Jesus may be saying this sarcastically, as if to say, "You
Pharisees don't see yourselves as spiritually sick, so you don't
think you need a doctor." If that is correct, then Jesus is
implying these sinners who are heeding His message are
humble enough to view themselves as sinful people and seek
God's forgiveness, but not the Pharisees, for they don't think
they need it. Is not the church of Jesus Christ full of Pharisees,
even in the twenty-first century? Christ's rebuke of the
Pharisees continues:

> But go ye and learn what that meaneth, I will have mercy, and not
> sacrifice: for I am not come to call the righteous, but sinners to
> repentance. Matt. 9:13

Jesus quotes Hosea 6:6, *I will have mercy*. That is, God
wants mercy, an inward attitude of graciousness toward

others. He does not merely want sacrifice or external religious rituals. Jesus came to call humble sinners to repentance, those who have a heart of mercy toward others, not arrogant Pharisees, who have no mercy. The Pharisees were unwilling to forgive others. Dear Christian, don't be like the Pharisees! Don't be unforgiving! Don't be judgmental or condemning! Don't be condescending or hypocritical! Don't be unmerciful! Because if you continue in these inward attitudes, you will be relegated to the darkness outside. You will be on the outside of his heavenly Jerusalem, the ruling realm of the Messianic kingdom, wishing you were inside.

Oh, that you might cast yourself at the feet of your king and cry out now for His mercy! *Blessed are the merciful: for they shall obtain mercy*, Matt. 5:7.

---

[8] R.T. France, *The Gospel of Matthew. The New International Commentary on the New Testament Series.* (Grand Rapids: Wm. B. Eerdmans Publishing Co., 2007), p. 706.

[9] Thomas Constable, *Dr. Constable's Notes on Matthew* (.pdf version, 2016 edition), p. 135.

Chapter 14

Humble as Children

Parables of the Lowly Seat and the Pharisee & Publican
Luke 14:7-14; 18:9-14

Some people always have to be first in line. They vie for the best seat. They long to be recognized and honored. They aspire to sit next to the movers and shakers. They want to have their picture taken with the high and lofty. Perhaps there is some of that innately in all of us. Jesus condemned this "me-first" attitude in a parable.

> 1 And it came to pass, as he went into the house of one of the chief Pharisees to eat bread on the sabbath day, that they watched him.
> 7 And he put forth a parable to those which were bidden, when he marked how they chose out the chief rooms; saying unto them,
> 8 When thou art bidden of any man to a wedding, sit not down in the highest room; lest a more honourable man than thou be bidden of him;
> 9 And he that bade thee and him come and say to thee, Give this man place; and thou begin with shame to take the lowest room.
> 10 But when thou art bidden, go and sit down in the lowest room; that when he that bade thee cometh, he may say unto thee, Friend, go up higher: then shalt thou have worship in the presence of them that sit at meat with thee.
> 11 For whosoever exalteth himself shall be abased; and he that humbleth himself shall be exalted. Luke 14:1, 7-11

Rebuke at the Chief Pharisee's House

In this parable Jesus does something unheard of. He rebukes the guests at a Pharisee's dinner party. Not to mention, the host is one of the *chief* Pharisees. It is culturally taboo to speak in such a critical manner to guests at someone else's private event. But Jesus cares not about cultural taboos. He cares about truth, and so He takes this opportunity to teach His countrymen that God is looking to reward humility, not self-exaltation.

Jesus notices how the guests seek out the best places to sit, the most advantageous, the closest to the host, without regard for others. They think themselves worthy of the honor. And so our Lord warns the guests that their self-exaltation will result in demotion. Only an attitude of genuine humility ends in promotion.

Clearly, Jesus has matters of reward and the heavenly kingdom in mind — look at the end of v. 14, *For thou shalt be recompensed* (i.e., repaid accordingly) *at the resurrection of the just*. Recompense is payback — whether good or bad — either promotion or demotion, ruling and reigning or the darkness outside. The purpose of this text is to clarify what God rewards. He does not reward a hoity-toity spirit of loftiness. He rewards a self-effacing, lowly and humble spirit.

Demotion for the High and Lofty

Notice how Jesus illustrates this principle to those in attendance — see vs. 8-9. How embarrassing it must be for those who take the honored positions at the dinner to have to be moved to a lower place by the host. I wonder if this will happen at the Judgment Seat to those who have the attitude that *all* Christians are overcomers and therefore inheritors, *all* will be rewarded, *all* can expect the wonderful blessings of glorification and crowns and positions of ruling, *all* will be in the immediate presence of Jesus forevermore. Isn't this a presumptuous spirit, especially when the Scriptures are so clear to the contrary?

Undoubtedly, many who have this attitude will be moved by Jesus to lower places, perhaps even removed to the darkness outside, to their shame and horror. Perhaps this is why John warned in 1 John 2:28, *And now, little children, abide in him; that, when he shall appear, we may have confidence, and not be ashamed before him at his coming.* What a foolish thing to posture your thinking to assume a prominent position will be yours in the kingdom. Is it not arrogant?

The right attitude is found in v. 10. Jesus tells the haughty, selfish guests, "You should rather take a lowly seat, then if the host decides to upgrade your seat to first class, you will be pleasantly surprised and honored by those who share the table with you." What can twenty-first century saints take away from this parable?

As we are striving for the mastery, we should be counting personal gains and achievements as loss for Christ. We should have lowliness of mind while pressing toward the mark, never having presumption of spirit that we have arrived. For the moment we think we have arrived, we can be sure we have not. Thinking we have arrived is akin to the idea of being humble and proud of it. It's rather foolish.

Lowliness of mind characterized Jesus.

> He is despised and rejected of men; a man of sorrows, and acquainted with grief: and we hid as it were our faces from him; he was despised, and we esteemed him not. Surely he hath borne our griefs, and carried our sorrows: yet we did esteem him stricken, smitten of God, and afflicted. But he was wounded for our transgressions, he was bruised for our iniquities: the chastisement of our peace was upon him; and with his stripes we are healed. Isa. 53:3-5

> (He) made himself of no reputation, and took upon him the form of a servant, and was made in the likeness of men: And being found in fashion as a man, he humbled himself, and became obedient unto death, even the death of the cross. Phil. 2:7-8

Promotion for the Humble

Exaltation follows humility. This is the critical principle we must learn.

> Therefore will I divide him a portion with the great, and he shall divide the spoil with the strong; because he hath poured out his soul unto death. Isa. 53:12.

Wherefore God also hath highly exalted him, and given him a name which is above every name: That at the name of Jesus every knee should bow, of things in heaven, and things in earth, and things under the earth; And that every tongue should confess that Jesus Christ is Lord, to the glory of God the Father. Phil. 2:9-11

But we see Jesus, who was made a little lower than the angels for the suffering of death, crowned with glory and honour; that he by the grace of God should taste death for every man. Heb. 2:9.

Jesus humbled Himself, and God exalted Him. In like manner, if you will humble yourself, you will be exalted. Exaltation is reward at the Judgment Seat.

For whosoever exalteth himself shall be abased; and he that humbleth himself shall be exalted. Luke 14:11.

Be clothed with humility: for God resisteth the proud, and giveth grace to the humble. Humble yourselves therefore under the mighty hand of God, that he may exalt you in due time. 1 Peter 5:5b-6

Child-Like Humility and Dependence

Jesus uses children to illustrate the humility-exaltation principle.

1 At the same time came the disciples unto Jesus, saying, Who is the greatest in the kingdom of heaven? 2 And Jesus called a little child unto him, and set him in the midst of them, 3 and said, Verily I say unto you, Except ye be converted, and become as little children, ye shall not enter into the kingdom of heaven. 4 Whosoever therefore shall humble himself as this little child, the same is greatest in the kingdom of heaven. 5 And whoso shall receive one such little child in my name receiveth me. 6 But whoso shall offend one of these little ones which believe in me, it were better for him that a millstone were hanged about his neck, and that he were drowned in the depth of the sea. Matt. 18:1-6

13 And they brought young children to him, that he should touch them: and his disciples rebuked those that brought them. 14 But when Jesus saw it, he was much displeased, and said unto them, Suffer the little children to come unto me, and forbid them not: for of such is the kingdom of God. 15 Verily I say unto you, Whosoever shall not receive the kingdom of God as a little child, he shall not enter therein. 16 And he took them up in his arms, put his hands upon them, and blessed them. Mark 10:13-16

Jesus is not speaking about matters of salvation. Rather, He is speaking of sanctification leading to reward. The simile He uses is clear. <u>To qualify for inheritance in the kingdom, you must be as a little child — humble and dependent</u>. Little children are not able to do anything for themselves to sustain life. They are completely dependent on others, and that requires humility of spirit.

We tend to superimpose our human views of maturity on spirituality. For instance, in everyday life we teach those who are most dependent (infants and young children) to mature into independent adults. Spiritual maturity is actually the opposite — independent adults learning to humble themselves and mature into God-dependent children.[10]

So often we think we can do it on our own, and we neglect the Lord's help. That is when we spurn His grace and end up falling. For God resists the proud, but He gives grace to the humble (James 4:6). Oh that we might be like little children, humble and completely dependent on the help of our Lord for growth and victory in our spiritual walk!

> 24 And there was also a strife among them, which of them should be accounted the greatest. 25 And he said unto them, The kings of the Gentiles exercise lordship over them; and they that exercise authority upon them are called benefactors. 26 But ye shall not be so: but he that is greatest among you, let him be as the younger; and he that is chief, as he that doth serve. 27 For whether is greater, he that sitteth at meat, or he that serveth? is not he that sitteth at meat? but I am among you as he that serveth. 28 Ye are they which have continued with me in my temptations. 29 And I appoint unto you a kingdom, as my Father hath appointed unto me; 30 That ye may eat and drink at my table in my kingdom, and sit on thrones judging the twelve tribes of Israel. Luke 22:24-30

Advice for the Chief Pharisee

Once again we find the requirement of humility and servitude if we would inherit the kingdom. On that note, let us return to our opening text in Luke 14.

> 12 Then said he also to him that bade him, When thou makest a dinner or a supper, call not thy friends, nor thy brethren, neither thy kinsmen, nor thy rich neighbours; lest they also bid thee again, and a recompence be made thee. 13 But when thou makest a feast, call the poor, the maimed, the lame, the blind: 14 And thou shalt

be blessed; for they cannot recompense thee: for thou shalt be recompensed at the resurrection of the just. Luke 14:12-14

A chief Pharisee had invited Jesus to dinner, so Jesus addresses vs. 12-14 to this man. If I may paraphrase these verses, "Mr. Pharisee, don't hob-nob with big shots who have whatever life has to offer and who can repay your kindness by having you over to their house for dinner. Rather, reach out to those who are poor and handicapped and must rely on welfare to survive. By condescending to those folks in a spirit of humility and meekness, you will never be repaid by them, of course. But God will repay you at the Judgment Seat."

In Rom. 12:16, the apostle Paul admonished, *Mind not high things, but condescend to men of low estate. Be not wise in your own conceits.* That's the same idea Jesus is sharing in this parable.

The Prayers of the Pharisee and the Publican

We turn now to another parable that teaches the same themes, from a different angle.

9 And he spake this parable unto certain which trusted in themselves that they were righteous, and despised others:
10 Two men went up into the temple to pray; the one a Pharisee, and the other a publican.
11 The Pharisee stood and prayed thus with himself, God, I thank thee, that I am not as other men are, extortioners, unjust, adulterers, or even as this publican.
12 I fast twice in the week, I give tithes of all that I possess.
13 And the publican, standing afar off, would not lift up so much as his eyes unto heaven, but smote upon his breast, saying, God be merciful to me a sinner.
14 I tell you, this man went down to his house justified rather than the other: for every one that exalteth himself shall be abased; and he that humbleth himself shall be exalted. Luke 18:9-14

Please put out of your mind that this passage is referring to matters of salvation from condemnation. Once again, matters of sanctification are being discussed. That is quite obvious, given the context, the verses preceding and succeeding vs. 9-14 above. The first eight verses of Luke 18 are a parable about saints persevering in prayer. The verses following the parable of the Pharisee and the publican are parallel to what we already read in Mark's Gospel (Mark 10:13-16 — see above).

But Jesus called them unto him, and said, Suffer little children to come unto me, and forbid them not: for of such is the kingdom of God. Verily I say unto you, Whosoever shall not receive the kingdom of God as a little child shall in no wise enter therein. Luke 18:16-17

Clearly, the context is the kingdom of heaven and the matter of positive reward for faithful saints and negative reward for unfaithful saints. The passage continues in v. 18ff with the rich young ruler, which once again, is not about salvation or what we might call the *gift* of eternal life. It is about the *reward* of eternal life. In other words, the lion's share of this chapter is about the kingdom of the heavens. Therefore, we must interpret vs. 9-14 in this context.

Furthermore, the temple and its predecessor, the tabernacle, never represented salvation from eternal condemnation, but rather a place of sacrificing for renewing fellowship with God. The New Testament equivalent for saints is 1 John 1:7-9. Thus, the Pharisee and the publican praying in the temple, pictures communion with God. The problem is that one of these men has the wrong spirit for approaching God.

"God, I Thank Thee, That I Am Not as Other Men"

Notice the story line of the parable. A Pharisee and a publican go to the temple to pray. The Pharisee is haughty and condescending. He looks down his nose at the publican, thinking himself better. And why does he think he's better? Because he is not an extortioner or an adulterer or a thief like the publican. Any child of God could have a similar attitude. "Lord, I thank you that I am not like the drug dealer down on the corner or that drunk who stumbles out of the tavern. Lord, I thank you that I am not a homosexual or an adulterer." On and on we could go in our attitude.

Then the Pharisee goes on to gloat in his spiritual achievements — fasting twice a week, tithing, etc. Any twenty-first century Christian could do the same. "Lord you know that I read my Bible every day and go to church three times a week, and I tithe, and teach a Sunday School class. I even usher (guys) or work in the nursery (ladies). Others don't do that Lord, so I suppose I'm pretty good." Fundamentalists might add, "Why, I even have standards! I dress modestly and listen to conservative music, unlike those new evangelicals!"

As long as you compare yourself to someone who is really bad and sinful, or someone who doesn't live up to your standard or do as much "for the Lord" as you do, you will look pretty good. But it's arrogant to the core, and God hates that mentality. When you compare yourself to the Word of God, you will look really bad!

Incidentally, we know the Pharisees had things in order outwardly, but inwardly they were a mess — hypocritical and observing merely the *letter* of the law. That's why Jesus said to them:

> Woe unto you, scribes and Pharisees, hypocrites! For ye are like unto whited sepulchers, which indeed appear beautiful outward, but are within full of dead men's bones, and of all uncleanness. Even so ye also outwardly appear righteous unto men, but within ye are full of hypocrisy and iniquity. Matt. 23:27-28

"God, Be Merciful to Me a Sinner"

How different is the publican's attitude! *And the publican, standing afar off, would not lift up so much as his eyes unto heaven, but smote upon his breast, saying, God be merciful to me a sinner,* Luke 18:13. Publicans were *outwardly* sinful people and thus were looked down upon in the culture. After all, they collected taxes from Jews on behalf of the Roman government, lining their own pockets in the process. They were known as thieves, stealing from the people.

This publican is convicted about his sin. Undoubtedly, he has heard John the Baptist or Jesus or one of the disciples preaching, *Repent, for the kingdom of heaven is at hand*. He hangs his head in shame and repents of his sinfulness, crying out for God's mercy.

It is quite common for commentators to view this text as soteriological, relating to matters of salvation from eternal condemnation. They say these men are both unsaved. The Pharisee remains unsaved and the publican gets saved. I believe the context demands we take the position that both of these men are believers from the start of the parable. The Pharisee is a self-righteous believer, like many Christians today who think they are spiritually okay because they keep their list and don't sin outwardly like publicans and harlots. The publican is an outwardly profligate believer, living in transparent fleshliness, like so many Christians in our day.

Again, Jesus is not talking about matters of salvation; He is teaching about sanctification. The message He and John have been preaching (in the context of the Synoptics) is a message of repentance for believers, not salvation from condemnation for unbelievers. Notice also the conclusion of the parable is the same as in our previous parable: *I tell you, this man went down to his house justified rather than the other: for every one that exalteth himself shall be abased; and he that humbleth himself shall be exalted*, Luke 18:14.

You don't come to possess eternal life by being humble and crying out for God's mercy. Those are works. Salvation is by faith alone. This publican is an already-saved man who gets convicted about his sinful lifestyle and repents. He is not an unsaved man who comes to faith in Christ alone.

Justification by Faith vs. Justification by Works

Someone might ask, "Then why does v. 14 say, "This man went down to his house justified rather than the other? Isn't justification the language of salvation?" Actually, it depends on context. There are two types of justification. One relates to salvation, and the other relates to sanctification. Justification occurs positionally in your spirit when you believe on Jesus Christ alone for eternal life. You have been declared righteous by God because of Jesus Christ. On the other hand, justification occurs practically in your soul when you live righteously by appropriating your provision in Christ. Justification by faith alone results in the salvation of your spirit. Justification by works (after salvation) results in the salvation of your soul unto reward. Let's look briefly at the two and see how they are distinct.

> Being justified freely by his grace through the redemption that is in Christ Jesus.
> Therefore we conclude that a man is justified by faith without the deeds of the law.
> For what saith the scripture? Abraham believed God, and it was counted unto him for righteousness. Rom. 3:24, 28; 4:3

These verses refer to the salvation of your spirit when you believed on Christ for eternal life. Justification is by faith alone when it comes to salvation. But justification is by works when it comes to sanctification — Spirit-enabled works, but works nonetheless. James makes this point.

Abraham and Rahab Justified By Works

> Was not Abraham our father justified by works, when he had offered Isaac his son upon the altar?
> Likewise also was not Rahab the harlot justified by works, when she had received the messengers, and had sent them out another way? James 2:21, 25

Wait a minute! Didn't we just read in Romans that Abraham was justified by faith alone? How can James say Abraham was justified by works? Is this a contradiction? Not at all, there are *two* aspects of justification, as I've already said.

When was Abraham justified by *works*? When he offered Isaac on the altar. If that is referring to Abraham's soteriological salvation, then such salvation is by works. But that cannot be, for it is inconsistent with the preponderance of Scripture. So there must be another explanation. We can understand what is happening here in James 2:21 by understanding the chronology of Abraham's life. When did Abraham sacrifice Isaac? When He was an old man, well over one hundred years old. The event is recorded in Gen. 22. But when was Abraham justified by *faith*? Several decades earlier, when he believed God and God counted it to him for righteousness. That event is recorded in Gen. 15.

When was Rahab justified by *works*? When she hid the spies. Again, if that is how she was saved soteriologically, then salvation is by works. But we know that salvation by works cannot be equated with salvation by faith alone. So when was Rahab justified by *faith*? Some time earlier, for she shares her testimony with the spies in Joshua 2:9-11 regarding her belief in Jehovah God, and that had happened earlier in her life.

Thus, it is important to understand, there are two types of justification, not merely one. Justification is by faith alone with respect to salvation of the spirit, and justification is by works with respect to salvation of the soul, or sanctification, that results in reward at the Judgment Seat.

Back in our parable in Luke 18, after the publican repents of his sin to God, he goes home *justified*. In the context, this is justification of a practical nature, related to sanctification and the soul. The publican is now on the pathway of discipleship leading to reward because he is repentant and humble. The Pharisee is *not* on the pathway of discipleship, for he remains in his haughty, arrogant attitude, not seeing the need to repent. He will not inherit the kingdom of the heavens, nor will any child of God who is not humble.

The moral of the story, once again, is as in our previous parable: *Every one that exalteth himself shall be abased; and he that humbleth himself shall be exalted*, Luke 18:14. This reminds me of some of the Beatitudes. *Blessed are the poor in spirit: for theirs is the kingdom of heaven. Blessed are they that mourn: for they shall be comforted. Blessed are the meek: for they shall inherit the earth*, Matt. 5:3-5.

Do you have a humble heart? Or are you proud and haughty in spirit? Remember, your eternal reward is at stake.

---

[10] The observations of Pastor Todd Tjepkema, a personal friend, taken from private email correspondence dated Sept. 4, 2017.

Chapter 15

Making Eternal Friends

Parables of the Rich Fool and the Wasteful Steward
Luke 12:16-21; 16:1-13

Americans are rich. You may not think of yourself as wealthy, but that is because you are probably comparing your financial status to other Americans who are wealthier. But if you compare yourself to the people of the third world, you are quite well-to-do, even if you are in the lower class. Accordingly, Christ's parable of the rich fool is a tremendous warning not to lay up treasures on Earth. Rather, as children of God, we need to become *rich toward God* and lay up treasures in Heaven.

The Rich Fool

16 And he spake a parable unto them, saying, The ground of a certain rich man brought forth plentifully: 17 And he thought within himself, saying, What shall I do, because I have no room where to bestow my fruits? 18 And he said, This will I do: I will pull down my barns, and build greater; and there will I bestow all my fruits and my goods. 19 And I will say to my soul, Soul, thou hast much goods laid up for many years; take thine ease, eat, drink, and be merry. 20 But God said unto him, Thou fool, this night thy soul shall be required of thee: then whose shall those

things be, which thou hast provided? 21 So is he that layeth up treasure for himself, and is not rich toward God. Luke 12:16-21

It is quite common to hear preachers and Bible teachers gospelize this parable, claiming the rich man is an unbeliever who rejects the gospel, choosing instead to live what he deems to be the good life — money and possessions and pleasure and partying. In the end, he loses his soul, which they say, means that he goes to Hell. But that is not the correct interpretation. Jesus is speaking to His disciples about matters of sanctification and discipleship. This passage has nothing to do with salvation from eternal condemnation. Indeed, the context of the parable of the rich fool is directed to those saints who are already following Jesus in discipleship. *He began to say unto His disciples first of all*, Luke 12:1. Again, in Luke 12:22a, *He said unto His disciples*. Why do preachers gospelize this parable, along with so many other texts? Tradition dies hard.

The Vanity of Living for Here and Now

This parable is a warning for saved people, children of God, and what is the warning? In one sentence: Don't live for here and now! This rich man is clearly focused on making money. In his agricultural economy, that equates to barns and silos and grain elevators for storing *his fruits and his goods*, v. 18. This man needs more space for storing all his stuff.

In our economy, we might say his bank account keeps growing and he builds a bigger house, though it is not really necessary for living. And he builds more garages and sheds for storing his possessions. His focus is material, and his attitude is self-sufficient. *I will say to my soul, Soul, thou hast much goods laid up for many years; take thine ease, eat, drink, and be merry*, v. 19. There is no mention of God, no gratitude for God's provision. This man clearly views his property as *his own*, not God's. He does not have a stewardship mentality. Furthermore, he wants to live on easy street. He will eat and drink and be merry. Those things are not wrong of themselves, but this man is focused on them. He wants to live for pleasure — fine dining and pleasure as a way of life. Many Christians fall into this trap of covetousness, greed and materialism. Poor Christians are not exempt. Even those who are poor can have an attitude that longs for these things and works to attain them. And while you may not have gone to the extreme, as this man, you nonetheless struggle with the same temptations. Indeed, we have all been guilty of wasting God's resources at times and not living for eternity.

Notice God's warning to this rich fool. *Thou fool, this night thy soul shall be required of thee: then whose shall those things be, which thou hast provided?* v. 20. When death comes, which can be sudden and unexpected, then our stewardship is suddenly terminated, and it is accounting time. For this man, all he had lived and worked for went down the drain. He had nothing to show in the eternal realm. Lest we follow this man's lifestyle, we should take heed to the warning of the apostle Paul.

> For we brought nothing into this world, and it is certain we can carry nothing out. And having food and raiment let us be therewith content. But they that will be rich fall into temptation and a snare, and into many foolish and hurtful lusts, which drown men in destruction and perdition. For the love of money is the root of all evil: which while some coveted after, they have erred from the faith, and pierced themselves through with many sorrows. But thou, O man of God, flee these things; and follow after righteousness, godliness, faith, love, patience, meekness. 1 Tim. 6:7-11

What is the rich man's error? He laid up treasure for himself on Earth, rather than being rich toward God and laying up treasure in Heaven (v. 21). As a result, what will he have to show in the life to come? Nothing! He will be ashamed. He will weep and gnash his teeth, for he will undoubtedly be in the darkness outside of the bright ruling realm of Christ's city of reward. This man is a Christian, a child of God, who lives for the here and now and loses out at the Judgment Seat. God forbid that we should follow this man's example. We don't want to make choices like this man. Thankfully, Jesus gives another parable to help us avoid making the mistakes of the rich fool.

The Unjust Steward

> 1 And he said also unto his disciples, There was a certain rich man, which had a steward; and the same was accused unto him that he had wasted his goods.

2 And he called him, and said unto him, How is it that I hear this of thee? give an account of thy stewardship; for thou mayest be no longer steward.

3 Then the steward said within himself, What shall I do? for my lord taketh away from me the stewardship: I cannot dig; to beg I am ashamed.

4 I am resolved what to do, that, when I am put out of the stewardship, they may receive me into their houses.

5 So he called every one of his lord's debtors unto him, and said unto the first, How much owest thou unto my lord?

6 And he said, An hundred measures of oil. And he said unto him, Take thy bill, and sit down quickly, and write fifty.

7 Then said he to another, And how much owest thou? And he said, An hundred measures of wheat. And he said unto him, Take thy bill, and write fourscore.

8 And the lord commended the unjust steward, because he had done wisely: for the children of this world are in their generation wiser than the children of light.

9 And I say unto you, Make to yourselves friends of the mammon of unrighteousness; that, when ye fail, they may receive you into everlasting habitations.

10 He that is faithful in that which is least is faithful also in much: and he that is unjust in the least is unjust also in much.

11 If therefore ye have not been faithful in the unrighteous mammon, who will commit to your trust the true riches?

12 And if ye have not been faithful in that which is another man's, who shall give you that which is your own?

13 No servant can serve two masters: for either he will hate the one, and love the other; or else he will hold to the one, and despise the other. Ye cannot serve God and mammon. Luke 16:1-13

A steward has been accused of wasting his master's goods. He has been put on notice that very soon he must give an accounting. So he has only a short amount of time to get the books in order before meeting the master. How does this apply to children of God? As a child of God, you are His steward. But your stewardship will be terminated upon your death, as v. 2 says, *You may no longer be His steward.* God has put you on notice that a day of accounting is coming. You had better get your books in order. There is little time.

The Master intends for you to take heed to His warning and prepare to give a good accounting. Knowing that time is of the essence, how will you demonstrate that you have been faithful in using the master's resources? What cunning strategy will you employ to ensure that you will survive after your stewardship comes to an end? In the parable, Jesus shares the right strategy. Unfortunately, so many choose to ignore His counsel and pursue another Master.

Wasting God's Resources

All believers are stewards. God has entrusted to your care certain assets, and He intends that you use them for His glory, not for your own selfish consumption. The assets include health, family, time, talents, treasure (i.e., financial provision, in some degree), to name a few. Are you wasting God's resources? The word *wasted* (v. 1) in the Greek is the same word translated *wasted* in Luke 15:13, referring to the prodigal son who *wasted* his inheritance in riotous living. That is, he squandered his father's resources through loose living. What a disaster! But many Christians are doing the same in a little different manner.

What a tragedy to be given precious children by God and then squander the opportunity to raise them for His glory. What a tragedy to be given health and then ruin it through drugs or alcohol or a poor diet. What a tragedy to be given a mind and then destroy it by repeated wrong thinking. What a tragedy to be given some degree of financial provision and then squander it on foolish things — lottery tickets or excessive amusements, temporal things rather than eternal causes — laying up treasure on Earth rather than in Heaven. What a tragedy to be given a talent and never use it for the Lord. What a tragedy to be given twenty-four hours a day but squander it on foolish pursuits. That is what the steward does in this parable. He wastes his master's resources.

If you are a waster of God's assets, then you need to see yourself in the parable. Take heed, for the time of accounting is coming. What strategy will you employ to ensure that you survive after your stewardship comes to an end? The steward in the parable ponders this (v. 3), while awaiting his appointment with the Master. The man apparently considers himself too weak to succeed in a blue-collar career. Maybe he is old, or maybe he has gotten soft doing supervisory work for so long. He will not condescend to be a beggar. So he comes up with a plan — according to v. 4, he *resolves*. He makes a choice and determines to see it through. You must make a similar choice, by God's grace, to make *friends* who will receive you after your time of stewardship on Earth ends.

A Clever Plan

Notice what this steward does (see vs. 5-7). While still in the position of steward, he goes to those who owe his master money, and he discounts the amount owed. One debtor owes the master a hundred measures of oil, so he writes it down to fifty, a fifty percent discount. Another owes a hundred measures of wheat, and that is written down to eighty, a twenty percent discount off the debt. Needless to say, he makes friends very quickly.

How does the master respond? *The lord commended the unjust steward, because he had done wisely*, v. 8. To clarify, the "lord" is not the Lord Jesus Christ. It is the lord or master of the steward in the parable. While the steward's actions are unethical, the master is impressed with the cleverness of his employee to make long-term friendships and thereby preserve himself after the stewardship relationship is terminated. The master commends the steward for being resourceful.

Some have wondered why Jesus would use this steward as an illustration of our stewardship, seeing that the man did some unethical things. Is Jesus condoning the man's behavior? No, of course not! Is Jesus suggesting that we can somehow cut corners or do unethical things to get ahead in life? Absolutely not! It is important to understand that Jesus is only making *one* point of comparison, and it is found at end of v. 8, *The children of this world are in their generation wiser than the children of light*. What does this mean? The children of this world are the unsaved. The children of light are the saved. Here's the idea: Unsaved people tend to be wiser and more resourceful in laying up treasures on Earth than Christians are in laying up treasures in Heaven.

Friends of the Mammon of Unrighteousness

Jesus is in no way condoning worldly behavior. He is simply making the point that unbelievers are so driven in their use of money for temporal causes. Why aren't Christians as driven to use money for eternal causes? Our Lord then gives an admonition. *Make to yourselves friends of the mammon of unrighteousness; that, when ye fail, they may receive you into everlasting habitations*, v. 9. *Mammon* is wealth or money. It is called *mammon of unrighteousness*, not because money is evil, but because loving money is a root of all kinds of evil.

Many crimes are committed because of money, but saints can use money for good. Just as the steward in the parable made friends by using money to his advantage, so Christians should make friends, using money to their eternal advantage. How is this accomplished? By helping financially those Christian brethren who are in need, you will make friends for eternity. When you *fail* — that is, when you die and your stewardship is thereby terminated — you will have friends that will continue forever. Just as the steward used money to his advantage and made temporal friends who would outlast his stewardship, so you should use money and resources to your advantage by making eternal friends that will outlast your stewardship on Earth. Jesus told us how to do so:

> Then said he also to him that bade him, When thou makest a dinner or a supper, call not thy friends, nor thy brethren, neither thy kinsmen, nor thy rich neighbours; lest they also bid thee again, and a recompence be made thee. But when thou makest a feast, call the poor, the maimed, the lame, the blind: And thou shalt be blessed; for they cannot recompense thee: for thou shalt be recompensed at the resurrection of the just. Luke 14:12-14

God Uses Finances As a Test

The way to make friends for eternity is by giving to those in need, those who have no way of repaying your kindness. Jesus will make sure you are repaid at the Judgment Seat. *He that is faithful in that which is least is faithful also in much: and he that is unjust in the least is unjust also in much*, v. 10. God is watching how you use your money, and that includes your spending habits. But He is also watching how you give. If you are truly generous and giving toward eternal causes, then God considers that faithfulness in something of a little nature — *that which is least*. That kind of faithfulness will translate into a greater responsibility in the eternal realm, for God knows He can trust you with bigger things.

Don't miss this exciting principle: How you use your finances — whether for your own selfish earthly pursuits or for eternal causes — is a test that God uses to determine if He can trust you with bigger things. Those who fail in this (those who are *unjust in the least)* are unable to handle bigger, more important matters. *If therefore ye have not been faithful in the unrighteous mammon, who will commit to your trust the true riches?* v. 11. God cannot trust those who have been unfaithful in the area of finances with *true* riches, that is, eternal riches and responsibilities. He reserves the greater riches and responsibilities for those whom He knows use their money with eternal purposes in mind. If God knows you have not been a good steward on His behalf, why would He ever give you an eternal reward of your own? *And if ye have not been faithful in that which is another man's, who shall give you that which is your own?* v. 12. We carry the same character with us from this life into the next.

God or Mammon?

The climax of the parable is found in v. 13. *No servant can serve two masters: for either he will hate the one, and love the other; or else he will hold to the one, and despise the other. Ye cannot serve God and mammon.* You either serve God and His eternal cause, or you serve yourself and your own temporal causes. You can't serve both. When it comes to money, there is no such thing as split loyalty. If you love money and possessions in any degree, then those things are your master, not God.

Would God consider you faithful in your stewardship toward Him? One day soon your stewardship will end and an accounting will be given. Have you used your money and possessions for the purpose of making eternal friends who will welcome you into heavenly dwellings? Or have you used money and possessions for your own selfish temporal ends? *It is required in stewards, that a man be found faithful,* 1 Cor. 4:2. If you are faithful now in this small matter, then God will entrust to you greater riches in the age to come.

Chapter 16

Will He Find Faith on Earth?

Parables of Lending Loaves and the Unjust Judge
Luke 11:1-13; Luke 18:1-8

It is important to understand a Middle Eastern custom, not only prominent during the time of Jesus, but that also continues to this day in that region of the world. When guests are being entertained in a Middle Eastern home the host typically rolls out the "red carpet," doing his best to meet the needs of his guests. Food, drink, lodging and conversation will certainly be provided, and typically in abundance. This cultural expectation factors prominently in the parable before us.

> 5 And he said unto them, Which of you shall have a friend, and shall go unto him at midnight, and say unto him, Friend, lend me three loaves;
> 6 For a friend of mine in his journey is come to me, and I have nothing to set before him?
> 7 And he from within shall answer and say, Trouble me not: the door is now shut, and my children are with me in bed; I cannot rise and give thee.
> 8 I say unto you, Though he will not rise and give him, because he is his friend, yet because of his importunity he will rise and give him as many as he needeth. Luke 11:5-8

In this parable a guest shows up at midnight, of all times! Jesus is undoubtedly illustrating the unexpected nature of the visit and the inconvenience of it to the host. Nevertheless, cultural considerations obligate the host to provide for his guest's needs. The host is unprepared and so goes to his friend — perhaps a neighbor — at that late hour to borrow some bread. The first response of the neighbor is to say, "Go away! It's late and we're all in bed." Nevertheless, because of the host's continued asking (importunity), the neighbor gets out of bed and loans his friend as much bread as he needs to feed the unexpected guest. In the end, the needs are met, albeit reluctantly. The spiritual application is clear because Jesus states it plainly.

> 9 And I say unto you, Ask, and it shall be given you; seek, and ye shall find; knock, and it shall be opened unto you.
> 10 For every one that asketh receiveth; and he that seeketh findeth; and to him that knocketh it shall be opened.
> 11 If a son shall ask bread of any of you that is a father, will he give him a stone? or if he ask a fish, will he for a fish give him a serpent?
> 12 Or if he shall ask an egg, will he offer him a scorpion?
> 13 If ye then, being evil, know how to give good gifts unto your children: how much more shall your heavenly Father give the Holy Spirit to them that ask him? Luke 11:9-13

Having now seen the parable and its spiritual application, we can make three observations.

Observation #1. The purpose for asking is because our friend has a need and we are destitute of ourselves to meet the need.

Our ministry is always to others. Be they saved or lost, people need bread for their hungry souls. Jesus is the Bread of Life. Those who eat of His bread never hunger. We have no bread of ourselves with which to minister to others, so we must go to the Lord, asking Him to provide what is needed. Yes, we have the Word of God and that is a critical component in ministry. Indeed, it is our basis for ministry. However, in the passage, the bread is clearly not a reference to the Word, for when we ask our heavenly Father for "bread" for ministry, He gives the Holy Spirit, according to v. 13.

Thus, the need is for the Holy Spirit to breathe life into our ministry to others. Whether preaching to an audience or teaching in a classroom or speaking one-on-one — such as in witnessing and discipleship — when we ask, He always answers by providing Holy Spirit enablement. Dare we try to minister without Him? Many do, which means their ministry is of the flesh — in demonstration of man's wisdom (1 Cor. 2:4) — and, consequently, lacking in power and effectiveness. Ministry in the flesh is not only ineffective, it can even be counterproductive, for the letter kills, but the Spirit gives life (2 Cor. 3:6). Oh, how we must recognize our inadequacy to meet needs of ourselves! The apostle Paul said, *Not that we are sufficient of ourselves to think any thing as of ourselves; but our sufficiency is of God,* 2 Cor. 3:5.

Some may argue that since all Christians have the Holy Spirit living within, there is no need to ask for Him. That leads to a second observation.

Observation #2: The request is for Holy Spirit empowering, not for the Person of the Spirit.

Frankly, I don't think Scofield's note on verse 13 is correct. He comments, "To go back to the promise of Luke 11:13 is to forget Pentecost, and to ignore the truth that now every believer has the indwelling Spirit."[11] Scofield is suggesting that this promise was merely for the benefit of the disciples, pre-Pentecost. Those original disciples, he implies, could have asked for the *person* of the Holy Spirit to come, and could have claimed this promise, in fulfillment of Joel's prophecy. Now that we have the indwelling Spirit, it seems Scofield thinks it is futile to go back and claim this promise, for He has already come.

While I appreciate many of Scofield's notes, I believe he makes an exegetical blunder at this passage. He misses the fact that the definite article is absent before the words *Holy Spirit* in the original language. When that is the case in Greek, then the reference is to the *essence* or *operation* or *nature* of the person or thing rather than its identity. In other words, Luke here, using very precise Greek language, is not referring to the *person* of the Holy Spirit but rather to His *ministry* of helping and empowering. That brings great meaning to this promise for disciples of all ages. What Jesus is, therefore, promising is that whenever we ask God for Holy Spirit enabling, our heavenly Father will give it!

This means that empowering is not automatic, though it is always available, through the Spirit who lives within us. God wants us to demonstrate our humble dependence on Him by asking for power rather than assuming we have it. Perhaps if we did not have to ask, we would tend to grow self-sufficient, thinking the power to be inherently ours.

Promises are made by God with the intention that His children claim those promises, not spurn or ignore them. Yet I suspect that within modern Christianity this promise is largely forgotten, perhaps because Scofield has relegated it to first century disciples only. Maybe a college professor has done the same and thereby hurt the faith of his students, or perhaps a pastor to his church congregation. God forbid that we should ignore a promise of God, to our own peril! We come to a third observation.

Observation #3. The answer is always granted to those who ask in faith.

Verse 13 promises, *How much more shall your heavenly Father give the Holy Spirit to them that ask Him?* What are we to do with promises? Claim them; that is, believe them. If we truly believe this promise, then the moment we ask, we should consider it done. Take it by faith. For God, who has promised, cannot lie. He must fulfill His word.

How, then, does the idea of importunity factor into this parable? Importunity in asking God is the idea of boldness, persistence, and expectancy in our asking. It is faith that endures until the answer arrives. But doesn't the importunity, as presented in the parable, give the impression of an arm-twisting, cajoling, pestering mentality that won't stop until it gets what it wants? Is this parable intended to teach a "squeaky-wheel-gets-the-grease" philosophy of prayer? God forbid! Where's the faith in that? *That* kind of praying is meritorious, suggesting the more one pesters God, the more likely he is to get an answer.

While that may be the case in the *illustration* used in the parable — beating on the neighbor's door at midnight — it is certainly not the case in the *divine application* — asking God for Holy Spirit enabling for ministry. The parable shows the stark contrast between how man responds vs. how God responds.

Four Points of Contrast

a. The neighbor in the parable is asleep and must be awakened. In contrast, our God never slumbers or sleeps. He is always alert to our requests. He never rebukes us for asking, nor does He refuse to answer. He is always ready and willing.

b. The parable poses a friend-neighbor (peer) relationship, whereas with God we have a Father-child (family) relationship, the point of v. 13. If a neighbor will reluctantly loan his friend some bread after much arm-twisting, and if a sinful, earthly father will eventually fulfill the persistent requests of his children, *how much more* will God graciously give His own children Holy Spirit empowering when they ask for it in faith?

c. In the parable, the expectation is that the bread is a *loan* from the neighbor; it will need to be repaid. However, with God, His bestowal of the Holy Spirit's enabling power is granted out of His gracious heart.

d. The neighbor in the parable has made his friend no promises to loan bread when needed, but God has promised to empower us with His Spirit when we ask. The contrast is vivid between man and God. Man must often be pestered before reluctantly meeting needs, but not God. Indeed, it would be rank unbelief for us to pester God for His power when He has already promised it.

To be sure, there is a continued asking implied in vs. 9-10. The Greek verbs (ask, seek, knock) are in the present tense, which means continued action (*keep* asking, *keep* seeking, *keep* knocking). But this is not importunate arm-twisting or vain repetition. To continue asking, seeking and knocking is simply coming to God every time we need His power for ministry. We don't ask once and expect to have His power for the rest of our lives. Nor do we ask repeatedly to get his power for the immediate situation at hand.

Nullifying God's Power

Incidentally, is it possible to ask for God's power and not get it? Absolutely, in at least four situations:

1. When you have sin in your life. In that case, you are not a candidate for receiving the Spirit's power. Instead, you need to learn to walk in the Spirit and not fulfill the lusts of the flesh.

2. When you fail to see your own insufficiency. Verse 6 says, *A friend of mine in his journey is come to me, and I have nothing to set before him.*

3. When you selfishly want power merely for the sake of power, not for the purpose of ministering to others. Again, v. 6 says, *A friend of mine in his journey is come to me, and I have nothing to set before him.*

4. When you fail to depend upon God's promise in faith. The promise is put in the form of a question: *How much more shall your heavenly Father give the Holy Spirit to them that ask him?* v. 13.

Virtually every time I am about to preach or minister to others in some way, I pray quietly in this fashion. "Lord, I need your bread for hungry people now. Please empower me with your Spirit, as you have promised. I take you at your Word." I don't pray numerous times, just once. Then I go forward with complete confidence, knowing He has answered. Tomorrow, I will pray the same, when needed, and again the next day and the next, and so on. What is the result? He demonstrates His Spirit and power through my life, and I know it's not of me. Praise the Lord for His promise of empowering!

Has your speaking in the name of the Lord been in demonstration of man's wisdom or in demonstration of the Spirit and power? There is no middle ground.

Parable of the Unjust Judge

Knowing that God is always gracious to hear and answer our prayers, we should pray consistently, seeking our heavenly Father's help and guidance in all things. To encourage us to remain faithful in prayer, Jesus shares another parable:

1 And he spake a parable unto them to this end, that men ought always to pray, and not to faint;

2 Saying, There was in a city a judge, which feared not God, neither regarded man:

3 And there was a widow in that city; and she came unto him, saying, Avenge me of mine adversary.

4 And he would not for a while: but afterward he said within himself, Though I fear not God, nor regard man;

5 Yet because this widow troubleth me, I will avenge her, lest by her continual coming she weary me.

6 And the Lord said, Hear what the unjust judge saith.

7 And shall not God avenge his own elect, which cry day and night unto him, though he bear long with them?

8 I tell you that he will avenge them speedily. Nevertheless when the Son of man cometh, shall he find faith on the earth? Lu. 18:1-8

This parable troubles some students of the Scriptures. They wonder why God is compared to an unjust judge who does not fear God or care about people. The judge is a blatant violator of the Golden Rule. The only reason he grants the woman's request is because of her persistence. This woman is a nag! He wants to get rid of her, and the only way is by granting her petition. So he does.

How is God like this? The point is, God is *not* like this judge. The parable doesn't *compare* God with this judge; it *contrasts* God with this judge. This judge delays and refuses to answer unless pestered and nagged. God, on the other hand, answers *speedily* — as v. 8 indicates — when His children are always praying and not fainting in heart (v. 1).

Will He Find Faith in You?

The final sentence of this parable is a fitting way to close our book on the parables. *When the Son of man cometh, shall he find faith on the earth?* Jesus is coming again, first in the clouds to rapture up His church, and then to Earth to defeat the enemies of God and establish His kingdom in righteousness. He is looking for faithful saints to rule together with Him — those who are full of faith. What better way for us to demonstrate faith than by praying watchfully? Prayer demonstrates that we are insufficient of ourselves and dependent on God for strength, guidance, wisdom, protection, provision, etc.

Is the twenty-first century church of Jesus Christ characterized by faith-filled saints? When He returns, will He find faith
on Earth? Faith is essential to reward. For it is only by faith
that we appropriate God's grace, and it is only by God's grace
that we can accomplish works that glorify Him.

I want to qualify to rule as the co-regent of Jesus in His
coming Messianic kingdom. I'm sure you do as well, or you
would not have taken the time to read this book. Thank you
for reading. May the Lord prepare you to reign with Him in
righteousness from His heavenly city!

---

[11] C. I. Scofield, *The Scofield Reference Bible* (Oxford: Oxford
Univ. Press, 1945), 1090.

Scripture Index

Made in the USA
Middletown, DE
19 November 2017